INKLE LOOM WEAVING

INKLE LOOM WEAVING

BY NINA HOLLAND

WATSON-GUPTILL PUBLICATIONS, NEW YORK

PITMAN PUBLISHING, LONDON

First published 1973 in the United States by Watson-Guptill Publications,
a division of Billboard Publications, Inc.,
1515 Broadway, New York, N.Y. 10036

Published 1974 in Great Britain by Sir Isaac Pitman & Sons Ltd.,
39 Parker Street, London WC2B 5PB
ISBN 0-273-00406-9

Library of Congress Cataloging in Publication Data
Holland, Nina, 1934-
   Inkle loom weaving.
   Bibliography: p.
   1. Hand weaving. I. Title.
TT848.H58   1973   746.1's   73-5758
1973   746.1'4   73-5758
ISBN 0-8230-2551-9

Manufactured in U.S.A.

First Printing, 1973
Second Printing, 1974
Third Printing, 1976

Acknowledgments

Special acknowledgment is due to Thomas Holland, my husband, who not only did the black and white photography, but also liberated me frequently from household chores so I could work on this book.

Appreciation also goes to Robin Brown, who did all the color photography and the technical work of developing and printing the black and white photographs.

Additional acknowledgment is due: Randy McMillian for his photographs of the hanging by Marilyn Leon, Project 13; Mihoko Matsumoto for her photograph of her hanging, Project 13; Indiana University Audio Visual Department for their photographs of the works of Terry Illes, Project 13; and the Henry Francis du Pont Winterthur Museum in Delaware for their photograph, Chapter 2.

Contents

An inkle loom belt woven by Andrew J. Perel, age 12, under the watchful eye of his art teacher, Ms. Arlene Olshak of the South Orangetown Jr. High School, Blauvelt, N.Y. The belt was woven of 4-ply wool in blue, red, and orange.

Introduction

The inkle loom is an excellent introduction to handweaving. It's inexpensive, versatile, and employs both simple and sophisticated techniques. You'll learn to produce a belt in less than an hour. Even the simplest weaving projects can have a unique design and be of professional quality.

This book is written for students, teachers, homemakers, therapists, and recreational directors—all those who wish to get started in weaving on their own. It's written for you.

Almost anyone who learns the craft agrees that there's a great satisfaction in making something useful, unique, and beautiful. The practical person may emphasize the function of his design; the home planner, its decorative qualities; the artist-craftsman, its expressive possibilities. For many, inkle weaving is a combination of these qualities. Others simply enjoy using their hands as well as the rhythm of movement in the act of weaving.

Our culture today is taking a closer look at its sense of values. With this look comes a renewed appreciation for that which is well made by man, whether it's for the sake of art, utility, or decoration. A new popularity in weaving is developing. One statistician claims there are 200,000 handweavers in the United States and Canada. Another survey indicates that over 80,000 people own some type of handloom.

The question is, how to get started and what to make. The sequential projects in this book will, I hope, offer a solution. The projects are intended to introduce techniques and design possibilities on a step–by–step basis. First you'll learn how to make a loom, then how to weave on it. A horseman from New Mexico claims he learned to ride from a book—the book was in one hand, the reins in the other. His collection of blue ribbons proves he learned his lessons well. Weaving is certainly as easy to learn.

With the completion of each project you'll have products to enjoy or perhaps even sell. Although it would be unfair to feature the craft as a means of support, many weavers will find a market for their products. A Vermont weaver, true to her Puritin heritage, says her handweaving always pays at least for her yarns.

You'll see how the designs can be varied to your own liking, and that the ideas presented are merely a stepping-off point for your own creative interpretations. Think of the projects as basic recipes and season to taste.

You'll also become aware of the relationship between the purpose of the project and the materials and techniques you choose. No emperor's new clothes here. If a fabric needs to be strong, what yarns will you choose? If it needs to be soft, what yarns will you choose? Should you make a close weave or a tight weave?

Inkle weaving is a medium in itself, but it also provides a good starting point for weaving in general. The accumulated knowledge from the book and your experiences will provide an excellent backlog of information if you later wish to learn to weave on a

The fabric of this skirt was inspired by the inkle belt shown next to it.

four-harness loom or the large floor looms. If you know how to drive a car, driving a truck isn't that much more difficult. If you do wish to learn how to weave you'll still find many uses for your inkle, such as creating designs for warp face fabrics. Sometimes a spectacular belt design or color combination can be interpreted into a repeat for a large fabric. The terminology, the discussion of yarns, the design problems and techniques, all apply to many forms of weaving.

What is an inkle? All dictionaries agree that it's some kind of tape. For our purposes it's a band, belt, tape, or any woven strip that's long and narrow. Dictionaries don't agree, however, on the derivation of the word inkle. The Oxford English Dictionary suggests Dutch as the parent language. Some early English variations of the word it cites are: ync(h)ull, ynkell, ynkle, ynckle, inckle, incle and inkle.

Early recorded examples of inkle in our language now seem humorous. 1541: "For a pece or brode yncull for gyrdlls. . . ." 1567: "With baskets . . . on their arms, where in they haue laces, pynnes, nedles, white ynkell." Even in Shakespeare's *The Winter's Tale* Autolycus says, "Hath ribbons of all colors i' the rainbow, point . . . inkles, caddysses, camricks, lawnes."

So we see that some form of the word inkle has been in our language for over 400 years. The necessity for tapes and bands has a much longer history. From camel girths to border designs, narrow bands have been created by man for thousands of years.

Inkle or tape looms were often a furnishing of colonial living rooms. Here period apparel such as stay laces, suspenders, glove ties, hair laces, caddises, ferretings, and points were crafted at home.

Cultures from Asia to South America to Europe have invented methods of producing tapes, many of which have similarities in design and function. The inkle loom designs in this book combine useful ideas from several of these sources. You'll notice in the photographs that several loom styles are used to illustrate the weaving techniques. Examine carefully the different styles and then build your own inkle loom.

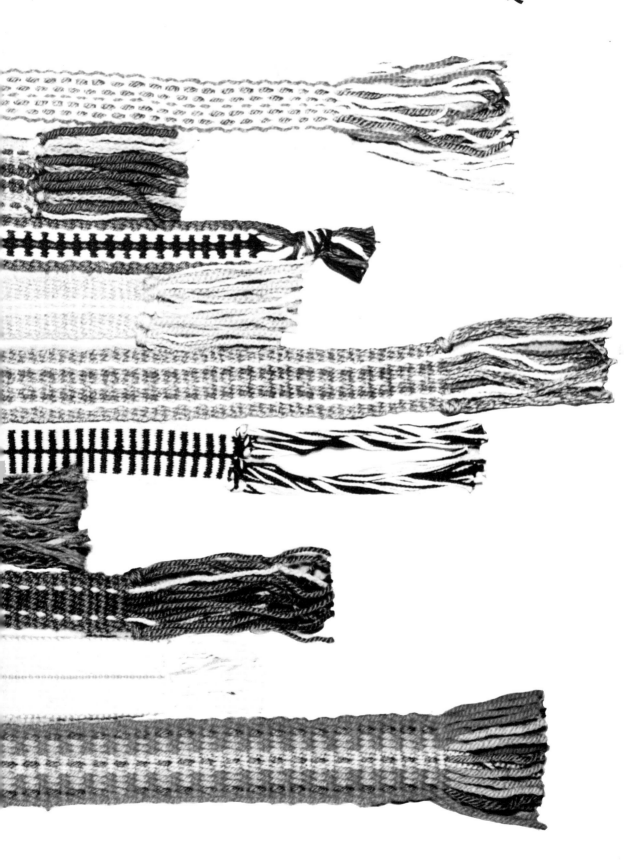

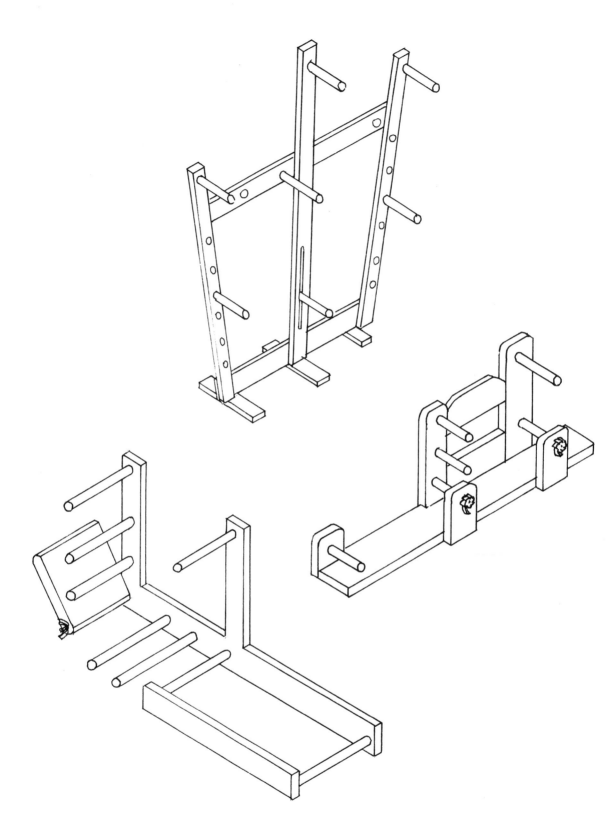

Three ready-made inkle looms: top, Leclerc (this is also convertible into a warping board); bottom left, Loom and Toy Factory; bottom right, Gilmore.

Building an Inkle Loom

Owning the right kind of inkle loom is essential if you want to weave quality projects. If you follow the instructions given in this chapter for building your own loom, you'll find your home-made loom will have several advantages not found in available models. It's made with accessible materials and tools and you need no great carpentry skills to put it together. It is also inexpensive: at the writing of this book, materials cost less than $5.00. Because of its size, the loom will handle, move, and store easily. It can accommodate belts up to 75″ long.

If you wish to build a loom for wider fabrics or longer belts, Chapter 2 offers alternative plans. If you're a more experienced carpenter, you may prefer to use other solutions for the tension adjustment. Several of these ideas are also discussed in the following chapter.

Before you start to build a loom, you may want to consider buying one to save the time it takes to build one. Many manufactured

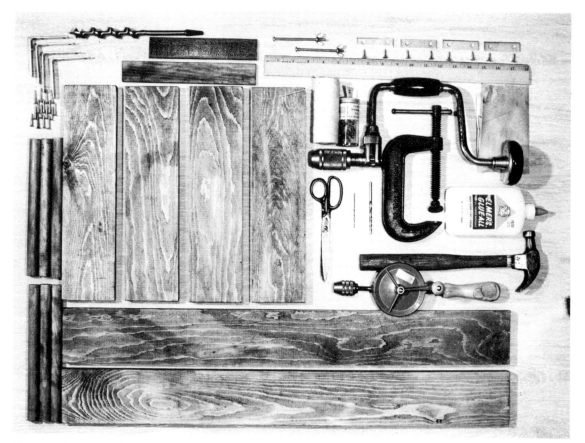

Here are the materials you'll need to make an inkle loom. All the items in the list on the following page except the screw driver, are shown here.

looms are made of hardwood, which provides an especially sturdy loom and is often a nice piece of furniture. If you do shop for a loom, be sure that it makes bands at least 48″ long. Looms may be purchased at prices ranging from $6.00 to $20.00. The more expensive ones are generally sturdier and allow longer bands to be woven. The drawing opposite illustrates three different models. Suppliers of looms and other equipment are listed at the end of this book.

If you have decided to save a few dollars—and also the time it takes to order a loom—then build your own. It's so simple that the proverbial "all thumbs" housewife or an enthusiastic eighth-grade boy can put it together.

Materials

The materials and tools needed to make your inkle loom are:

1. Two 1″ x 4″ x 30″ boards
2. Four 1″ x 4″ x 14″ boards
3. One 1⅝″ x ¼″ x 7¼″ lattice molding
4. One 1⅝″ x ¼″ x 9″ lattice molding
5. Six ¾″ x 9″ dowels
6. Two 3″ x ⅛″ carriage bolts with wing nuts to fit
7. Sixteen #6 ⅝″ screws
8. Eight #8 ⅝″ screws
9. Four 2½″ x ⅝″ bent corner irons
10. Four 2½″ x ⅝″ mending plates
11. Wire brads
12. String
13. Brace or electric drill with 3/32″, 3/16″, and ¾″ bits
14. Hand drill
15. One 4″ C-clamp
16. Scissors
17. Measuring stick
18. White glue
19. Sandpaper
20. Hammer
21. Screw driver

Please note that 1″ x 4″ lumber, cut at the lumberyard, is actually 13/16″ thick and 3⅝″ wide. The following directions use these dimensions. Examine all the steps used to build the loom before you start.

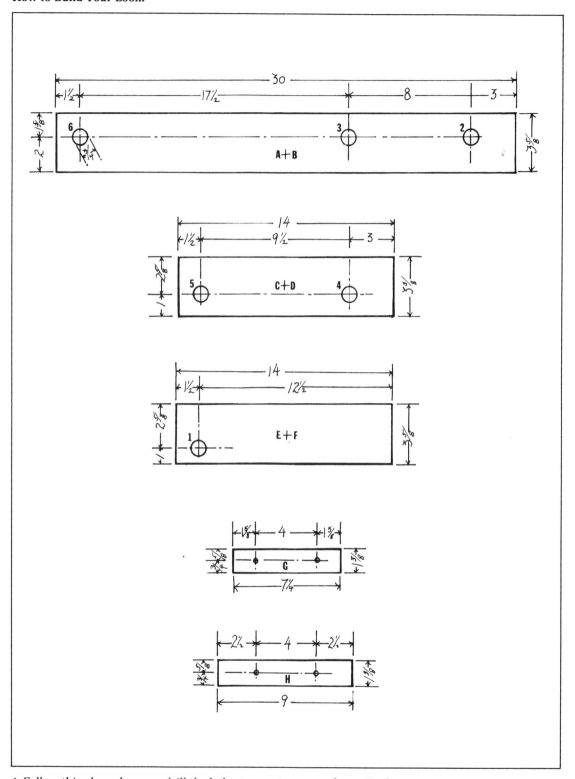

1. Follow this plan when you drill the holes to construct your loom. Each letter represents a board. For instance, you will drill two boards, E and F, according to the plan at the top. Use the dimensions illustrated to mark the center of each hole to be drilled.

2. Follow the plans diagramed in illustration 1 to measure and mark each board. Do this carefully so that the holes will line up when you put the pieces together.

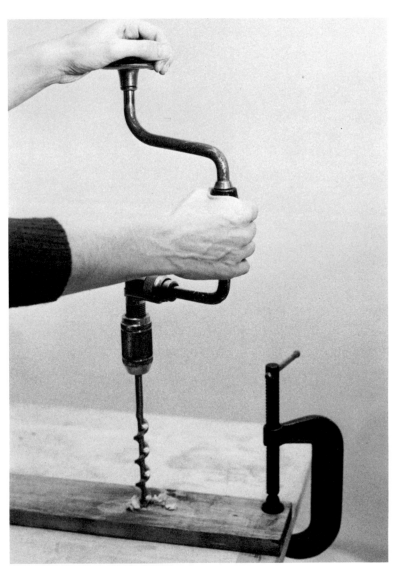

3. Drill ¾″ holes in boards A, B, C, D, E, and F at the points designated in illustration 1.

4. Drill 3/16″ holes at the points shown on boards G and H in illustration 1.

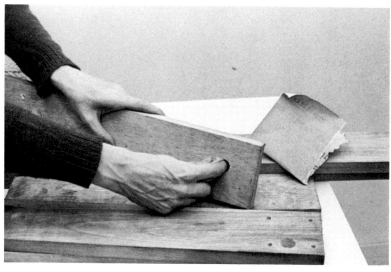

5. Sand the insides of the ¾″ holes so that the dowels will slip easily into place. Sand lightly over all surfaces of the boards and the dowels.

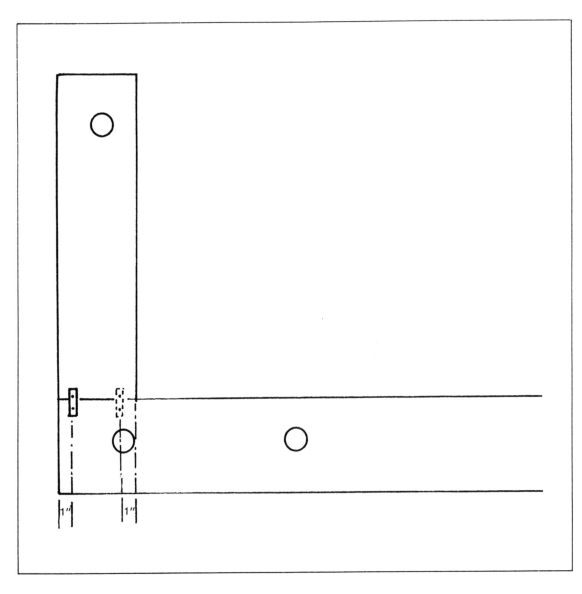

6. (Above) Place board E, with the ¾″ hole at the top, above board A near hole 2. Use the mending braces to join these two boards.

7. (Right) Mark the screw holes 1″ from the right side of board E for the placement of the screws.

8. Drill 3/32″ holes first, so that the screws will go into the wood without splitting it.

9. Glue the bottom of board E as shown.

10. Screw on the mending brace.

21

11. Flip the board over. Using the mending braces as a guide to center the holes, mark and drill 3/32″ holes 1″ from the right side of board E. This will stagger the braces on either side of the board. Then screw the brace into position. Join boards F and B in the same way.

12. To join board C to board A, mark, drill, and screw on one bent iron on either side of board C. The bottom of the iron should be in line with the bottom of board C (the #4 hole end).

13. Glue the bottom of board C. Mark, drill, and screw board C in place. The back edge of board C should be 9″ from the back edge of board A. Follow Steps 12 and 13 to join boards D and B.

14. Slip the six 9″ dowels into all the holes. You should be able to slip dowel #2 in and out easily because it's sometimes necessary to remove it while weaving. You may wish to do some additional sanding on this dowel. The other dowels should fit firmly enough to hold the loom rigid, but not so tightly that they can't ever be removed.

15. If the dowels don't fit firmly, jam some yarn into the hole with the dowel.

16. When the dowel is in place, cut off the yarn ends.

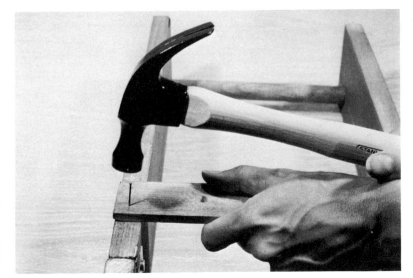

17. Attach the 1⅝" lattice molding to the back of E and F with the wire brads. The bottom of the molding should be 5" from the bottom of the loom.

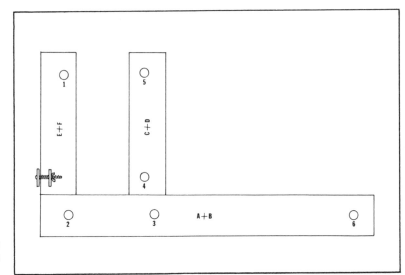

18. This diagram shows the placement of the lattice molding.

19. You may stain and varnish the loom if you wish.

20. Put carriage bolts through the holes and attach the 1⅝″ x ¼″ x 7¼″ lattice molding. You don't need to screw the wing nuts on tightly, because this is your tension adjustment. Now you have your finished loom. The next step is to make the heddles, or string loops, that you see in this photo.

Adding the Heddles

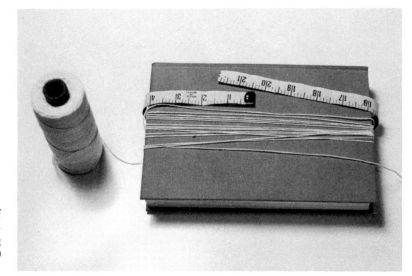

1. Find a book or a piece of stiff cardboard 20″ in circumference and wrap the string around it 50 times to make 50 complete cycles.

2. Cut through the strings at one point, so that you have 50 pieces of string, each 20″ long.

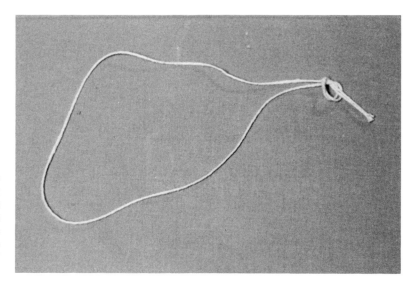

3. Tie the ends of each piece of string together so that it makes a loop. Make the knots as close to the end of the string as possible. Try to make all the loops the same size (a little less than 10″ long). Make 50 of these loops.

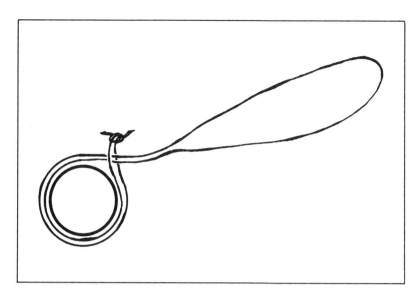

4. (Left) Put the loop around bar 3 by placing the knotted end toward you. Pass the loop back, then around the bar, and up under the knot.

5. (Below) Attach all the loops, or heddles, and your loom is complete.

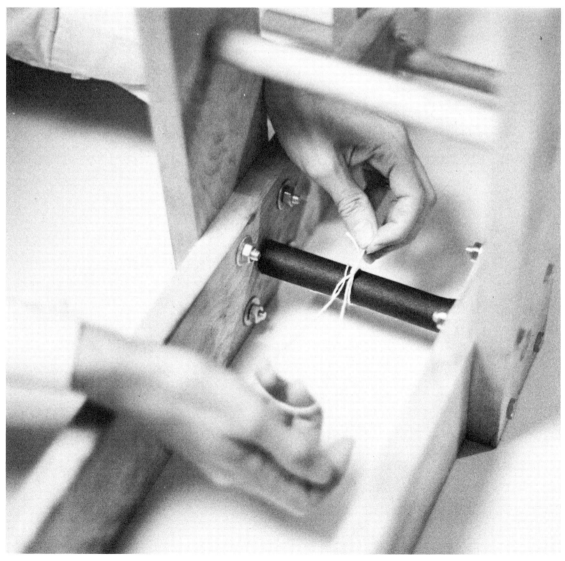

2 Alternative Loom Plans

The basic design for building an inkle loom has many possible variations. As you decide which design you wish to make, consider the following: the materials, the tools, and the woodworking skills you have to work with; what kinds of projects you wish to create; and the storage space you have for your loom.

Variations in Width and Length

The first variation to consider is the width of the loom. This is determined by the length of the dowels and is a simple change. To add width, simply increase the length of all the dowels and the tension adjustment bars at the back of your loom. The advantage is that you can weave wider projects such as scarves and placemats.

The second variation is for length. You can add two additional dowels 9" from the bottom of the loom at points #7 and #8. By zig-zagging the warp after it passes point #1, around #8, then #7, then #4, and continuing on the same path as before, your length will be extended 28".

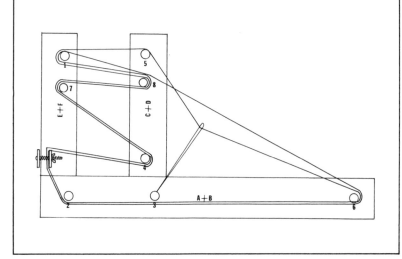

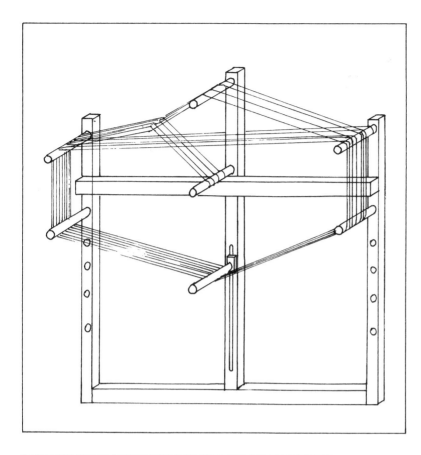

Another solution for added length is illustrated by the English-style loom. Here, three upright bars hold the various pegs. These upright bars are longer than those in the basic design and are braced by two horizontal bars. In this sketch, 1″ x 2″ hardwood is substituted for pine. The hardwood allows support for the bars and tension which will be upon them from the warp yarns. The facing uprights are not used in this plan, which allows for speedy warping.

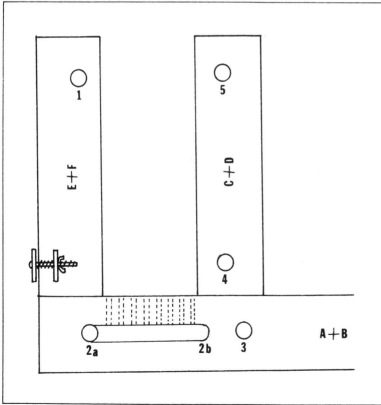

Adjusting Tension

For the basic design illustrated in Chapter 1, you need the least amount of carpentry skills and tools. If you're a skilled carpenter, you may prefer one of these ideas for the tension adjustment. Drill an extra hole in line with hole #2 9″ from the end of the loom. Now hollow out a ¾″ area between 2a and 2b with a saber saw or keyhole saw. Drill ⅝″ holes every ⁵⁄₁₆″ above the slot and down to it. Cut two ¼″ dowels 4″ long and place them in the holes, then slip the ¾″ tension dowels behind them.

This carpenter screwed his ¾″ dowels in place. This loom, therefore, looks a little different from the basic plan. To release the tension on your warp, remove the pegs, and replace them in the next pair of holes. Let the tension bar slip forward.

Some looms release the tension with a rounded 1″ x 2″ bar instead of a dowel at point #2. A hole the length of the bar is drilled through the center. A carriage bolt is slipped in the #2 position through the hole and a wing nut bolt holds it in place. When the warp is placed on the loom a 1″ x 2″ bar is in a position parallel to the floor. As the tension increases the bar is tipped upward, easing the tension.

Other Variations

Another variation requires a jig saw. Each F-shaped side of the loom can be cut in one piece from ¾″ plywood. In the photograph, the builder decided to chisel ½″ grooves between 2a and 2b. Five ¼″ holes were drilled 1″ apart along the groove. To hold the tension bar in place, ¼″ dowel pegs are used. The loom was painted in order to enhance the plywood.

These designs all use string heddles, but many weavers have used a hole–and–slot rigid heddle system instead. Colonial housewives frequently had a loom similar to this one ready to make tapes, with uses from shoe laces to hat bands. Photo courtesy of the Henry Francis du Pont Winterthur Museum, Delaware.

3　**Making a Shuttle**

A shuttle is a useful accessory designed to hold the weft yarn and to make passing it through the warp easier. The weaving directions in this book assume you'll simply use balls of yarn, but you'll find occasions when weaving would be easier with the aid of a shuttle.

To make your shuttle, cut a 10″ piece of lattice molding. With a coping saw, shape the corners so that they'll be curved, and cut elliptical holes from each end. Bevel one side with a scrub plane, shaping it into a dull wedge, as shown in the diagram. This will be useful to "beat" the yarn into place as you're weaving.

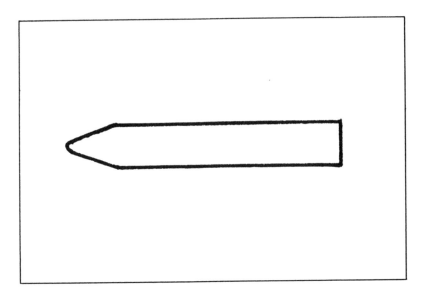

This illustration shows a cross section of the shuttle with one edge beveled.

To make a shuttle you'll need the materials shown here: a coping saw, a 10″ piece of lattice molding, and a scrub plane.

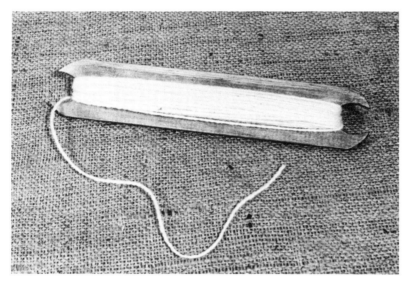

A finished shuttle, wound with weft yarn.

4   Shopping for Yarn

The first step in planning any weaving project is to shop for the proper yarns. Most weavers find only a few yarns available in local stores, and soon start accumulating yarn samples from various suppliers. There's a list of suppliers in the back of this book. If you mail them fifty cents and your address, they'll send you samples and a price list. A full and up-to-date file of samples is an asset when planning any project. Because it can take up to three weeks for yarn orders to arrive, do become acquainted with the yarns carried by your local stores. The five-and-dime store often has crocheting cotton which can be quite useful in the heavier weight.

Rug yarns can vary tremendously in fiber content, weight, and smoothness. Most rug yarns can be used on the inkle loom unless they are very loosely spun. Knitting yarns are usually difficult to work with as they have too much spring and when stretched on the loom quickly lose their tension.

Hardware stores carry an interesting assortment of cotton cord and jute, which can be useful for projects with a casual look. Although yarn shops sometimes carry weaving yarns, the merchant generally caters to the knitter, not the weaver.

The design of your weaving will be determined by the warp—the yarns that are strung on the loom. These yarns should be strong and smooth. Textured yarns do not make good warps: they eventually snag or break. Some good warp yarns are rayon, 2-ply wool, or 6-ply rug yarn.

These would be good warp yarns: rayon; 2-ply wool; 6-ply rug yarn.

These would *not* be good warp yarns. They are too uneven or rough.

A   B   C

For your first project, choose three colors of a rug yarn. All your colors should be of the same weight and fiber. You could use cotton or rayon blends, but wool is preferable because of its elasticity. The illustration shows 2-ply rug yarn. Roll each color into a separate ball, each about 2″ in diameter. These will be small enough to fit through the heddles and the tension adjustment.

5

Warping the Loom:
A Three-Color Belt

You are now ready to weave your first belt, which will have vertical stripes in three colors. You've already bought the yarns, so the first step will be to learn how to warp your loom. The warping procedure will basically be the same for any project that you'll weave on the inkle loom. Variations will occur mainly in the number of threads warped and in the sequence of colors.

Warping the Loom

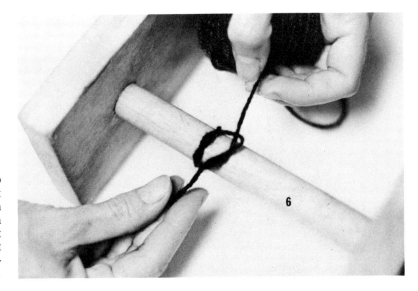

1. Tie the end of color A to bar 6. Use any knot that holds. Notice that the loom pictured is constructed with bolts and a slightly different dowel arrangement. Do not let this confuse you. The directions apply to your loom.

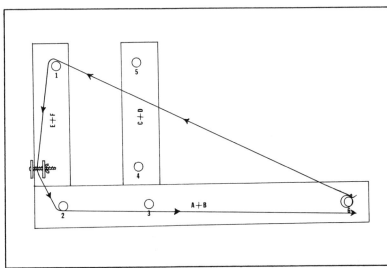

2. Pass the attached ball under bar 5, over bar 1, through the tension adjustment, under bar 2, under 3, and under 6. This is the first path.

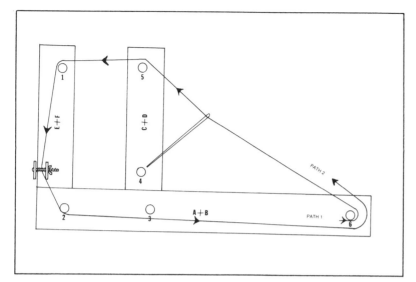

3. Now carry the same ball around bar 6, through the loop of the first heddle on the left, over bar 5, and around 1. Go through the tension adjustment, under bars 2 and 3, and back around bar 6. This is the second path. Note that you always put the yarn under bar 6.

4. Pull the yarn so the tension is loose, but not sagging.

5. Repeat this procedure, with the same ball of yarn, twice more. Be sure to go around the two paths alternately, and maintain your loose tension. You should have six warp strings, three going through the heddles, and three going directly to bar 1. Cut off the yarn after you've passed around bar 6, leaving 1″ extra at the end of the yarn.

37

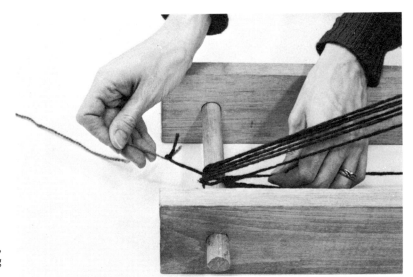

6. Tie on a new color, color B, to the end of color A, using any knot that holds.

7. Continue to string your warp threads. With color B, proceed going around the loom. Make four revolutions. You will have two strings on path 1, and two on path 2. Cut color B, and tie on color C. Remember to always cut all colors at bar 6. With color C, go around four times. Cut C and join A. With color A, go around twice. Cut A and join C. With color C, go around four times. Cut C and join B. With color B go around four times. Cut B and join A. With color A, go around six times and then cut color A.

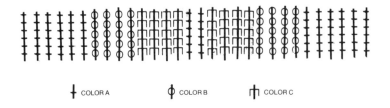

† COLOR A   φ COLOR B   ⊓ COLOR C

8. You should have a total of 30 warp threads. If you should run out of warp yarn before you finish a color, you may knot a new piece on, but always do it at bar 6.

9. Unknot your first string of color A from bar 6. Tie this to the end of the last string you warped. This will cross over the rest of the yarns, but it won't make any difference in the weaving. You have warped your loom.

10. Tighten the wing nuts so that your yarns are now under tension.

Weaving the Belt

1. Wrap some of color A into a 2″ ball. This is your weft yarn. The weft is the yarn you'll weave at right angles to the warp.

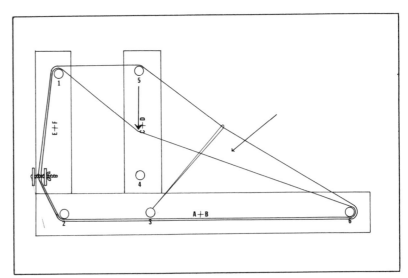

2. Tie the end of the weft yarn to the left side of bar 6.

3. Push down hard on the warp yarns that are below bar 5. This will separate the threads which run through the heddles from those which do not. The triangular space between the heddles and bar 6 is called *shed 1*.

4. Take a piece of 1″ x 5″ cardboard, and place this inside shed 1, about 4″ above bar 6.

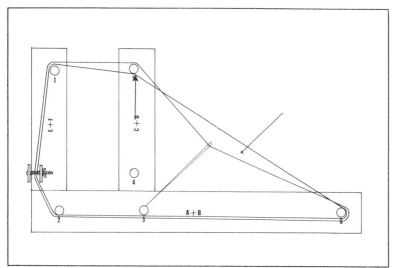

5. Now push the same threads up towards bar 5. This produces a new triangular space above the heddles, which is *shed 2*.

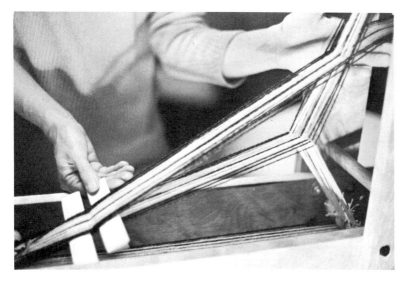

6. Place another piece of cardboard inside this shed. This will mark off the distance between the knots and the weaving for fringe. It will also give you something to push or "beat" your yarn against.

41

7. Produce shed 1 again. Take the weft yarn, from the left to right, through the shed. Push down firmly against the cardboard with your hand.

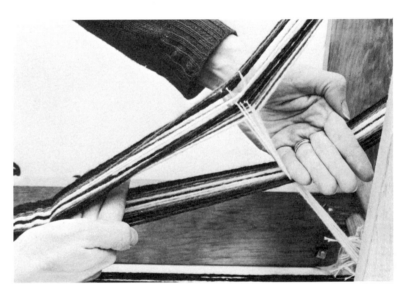

8. Change to the alternate shed. Keep all the warp yarns pulled together so the weft shows only at the edges. Weave the weft through from the right, pulling gently to the edge. Beat firmly into place with your hand. Repeat weaving back and forth in these two sheds. Try to keep both edges, or selvages, even. The illustration shows the weaving in progress with the hands holding shed 1 open.

9. When you've woven about 5", unknot the weft yarn from bar 6. Pull the warp yarns toward you, holding the yarns as illustrated. This will revolve the warp around the loom and give you unused warp to weave on.

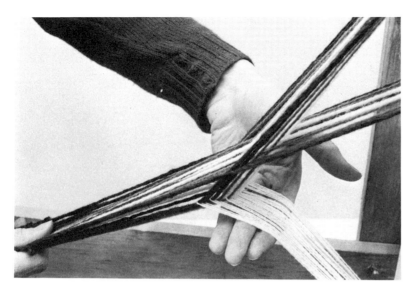

10. Slide the heddles back to their original position. Repeat the procedure of revolving the warp yarns after every 5″ of weaving.

11. If the warp yarns become too tight, unscrew the wing nuts a little at a time. This releases the tension. If this isn't enough, pull bar 2 out completely. Again tighten the wing nuts.

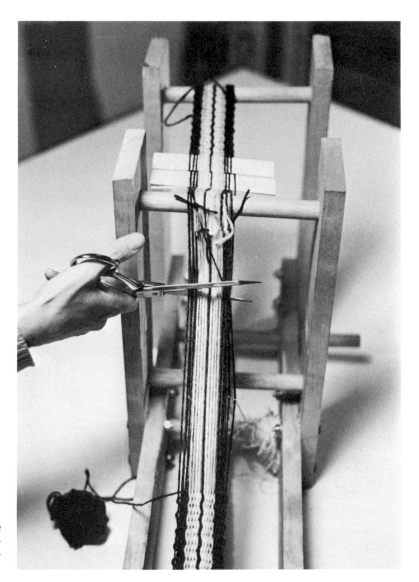

12. When all but 15″ have been woven, cut the unwoven threads 7″ from the beginning of the weaving.

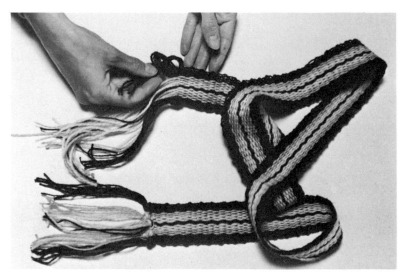

13. You can finish the ending fringe in one of several ways. One way is to knot every six threads together at the point of weaving.

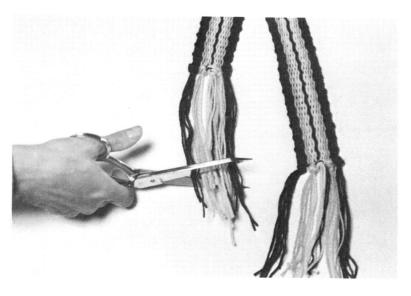

14. Trim the fringe evenly.

15. Another method is braiding the fringe. Macramé books may give you additional ideas for fringing (see Bibliography).

16. It's important to keep edges and fringes neat. This care can make the difference between an amateurish and a professional piece of work. A nice finishing touch is the addition of your own label. Label suppliers are listed in the back of this book, or an original design can be made by your local printer.

6 Yarn Texture: A Choker

Transform an old-fashioned style into a contemporary accessory—weave a choker. Because you won't want a coarse weave or scratchy fiber next to your skin, you should first explore the texture variance caused by different yarns. Yarns are composed of fibers that are twisted and pulled.

Wool. Weavers commonly prefer natural fibers. Wool is a favorite—it's elastic and regains nearly all its original shape after it's been under tension. Wool also dyes well, so many beautiful and brilliant shades exist. It's a good insulator and not highly inflammable. If tightly spun, it produces a strong yarn.

Cotton and Linen. Cotton is also a popular fiber. Although it's not as brilliant or elastic as wool, it's washable, strong, and comfortable against the skin.

Linen is the strongest of these fibers, but it takes dye poorly and has no elasticity. For these reasons it's not well suited to belt weaving. Jute and paper cord offer possible texture variations.

Synthetics. Each synthetic fiber has special properties all its own. Rayon is used often by handweavers and although it's not very

Here are many types of yarn suitable for inkle weaving.

elastic, it does take dye well and often adds a nice sheen to a woven piece.

Yarns. A tightly spun yarn is preferred for inkle weaving. Under the friction of weaving, a loosely spun yarn becomes fuzzy. Because of its elasticity, it also becomes too slack while being maneuvered in the weaving process. One way to judge the tightness of spin is to look at the angle of the fibers on the thread. The deeper the angle the tighter the spin. Fibers spun once are called singles. Two or more singles are almost always respun together to make plied yarns. A 4-ply yarn has four singles spun together. The size of the yarn depends on how many plies there are plus the size of each ply. The larger the size number the smaller the diameter of the yarn. Yarn sizes are designated by the number of the size and the number of plies. An 8/4 cotton is a #8 cotton spun into four plies.

Weaving the Choker

Inkle weaving requires a strong, smooth yarn, but the choice of fiber and size of yarn offers many possible weaving textures. For a different texture than that of your first weaving, experiment with cotton for your choker. Choose your own color scheme and width of stripes. Cotton rug warp 8/4 or pearle cotton #3 can be used.

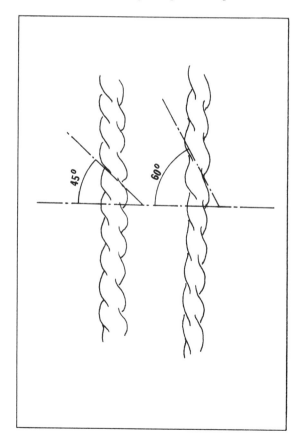

The angle of the fibers determines the tightness of the spin.

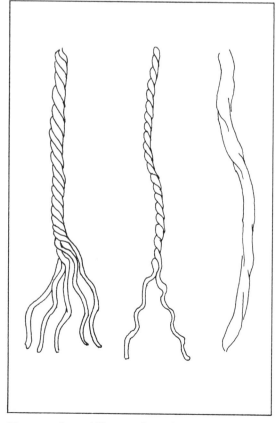

Here are three different plies of yarn.

Weaving the Choker

THROUGH HEDDLES

B	B	B	Y	R	R	Y	Y	B	Y	Y	R	Y	B	B	B
B	B	B	Y	R	Y	Y	B	Y	Y	R	R	Y	B	B	B

NO HEDDLES

B BROWN **Y** YELLOW **R** RED

1. (Above) To make a choker 1″ wide, plan for your weaving to have 32 warp threads. A piece of graph paper will aid you in planning. The top line will represent the threads which go through the heddles; the bottom line those that do not. This is called a draft. In the 32 blocks you can use crayons, colored pencils, magic markers, or an initial color code to plot your design. The draft shown is just one possibility.

2. (Right) Warp the 32 cotton threads, then measure 10½″ up from the knots for the fringe.

3. You'll immediately see the finer weave you're creating because of the size of the yarn. Feel the smooth character of the weave. You'll be able to weave two chokers on the length of warp on your loom. After you've woven a 12″ strip, insert a 3″ x 20″ piece of flexible cardboard or stiff paper into the length of the warp. This leaves enough warp for fringes on both chokers.

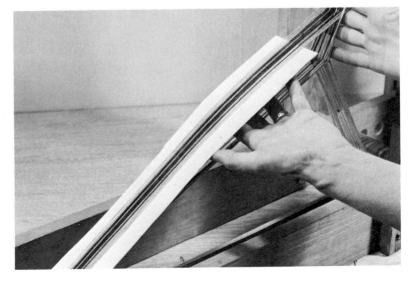

4. Now pick up the weft and start weaving again. Continue until you have another 12″ of weaving.

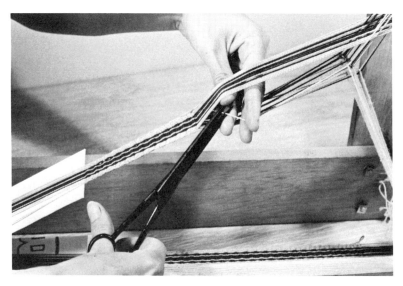

5. If you run out of weft yarn while you're weaving, cut the weft yarn so the end lies within the warp shed.

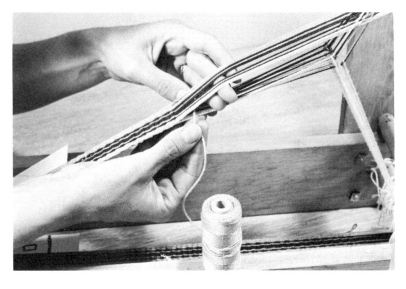

6. Insert the new weft in the same shed.

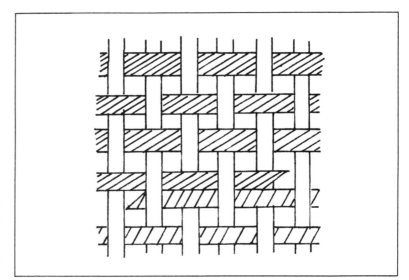

7. Let the new and old weft yarns overlap about ½" as shown in the diagram. Proceed weaving. This method avoids tying knots which would mar your work.

8. Continue until you have another 12" of weaving. Make one cut halfway between the two woven areas at the top of the loom.

9. Then make another cut, again halfway between the two woven areas, at the bottom of the loom.

10. Finish the fringe by making two braids on both ends of each choker for the ties. Your choker is complete.

7

Pattern Design: Tied Bodice Belts

A wide belt is a natural accessory for the peasant or gypsy look. Also traditional with colorful peasant blouses and full skirts are the busy patterns of "old-country" fabrics. Before you design a wide belt, you should explore the many pattern possibilities your inkle loom provides.

As you saw in the chapter on weaving a choker, patterns in inkle weaving are illustrated by drafts. The top line of the draft indicates the threads that go through the heddles. To the weaver, it represents one harness, or one group of threads, which is pulled up or down at the same time. The bottom line is another harness and doesn't go through the heddles. Codes usually designate the various colors of the yarns.

Patterns for Wide Belts

In this pattern a broken line runs the length of a solid color belt. It was done by introducing a single thread of a light color during the warping at two points.

The draft illustrates one portion of the band.

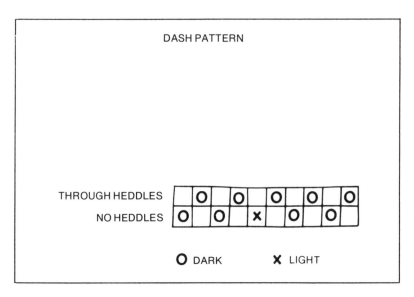

Horizontal stripes appear when all of the light colors are threaded through the heddles and all the dark colors are not. Note that a heavier weft was introduced in some sections, which makes the horizontal stripes a bit wider.

The draft shows how to warp the loom for a horizontal stripe.

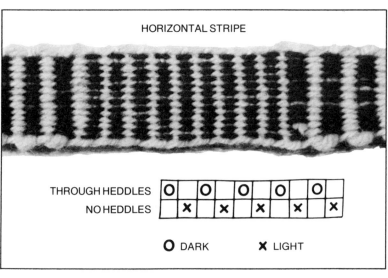

Instead of tying on each new color, you could leave the balls of yarn to the side at bar 6 when you're finished with them.

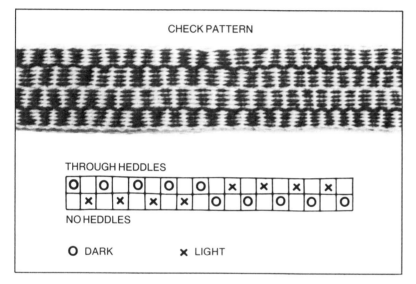

CHECK PATTERN

THROUGH HEDDLES

O		O		O		O		O		×		×		×		×	
	×		×		×		×		O		O		O		O		O

NO HEDDLES

O DARK   × LIGHT

You can get a checkered effect by first threading all dark yarns through the heddles for a few rounds, then switching and threading all light colors through the heddles. This method of threading is repeated across the belt until your belt is warped.

The draft shows how to warp the loom for a checkered design.

This photo shows the checkered design being woven on the loom.

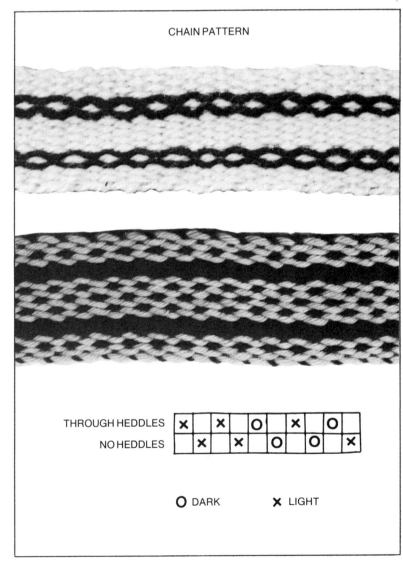

TEAR DROP PATTERN

THROUGH HEDDLES	O		X		O		O		X	
NO HEDDLES		O		O		X		O		O

O DARK   X LIGHT

CHAIN PATTERN

THROUGH HEDDLES	X		X		O		X		O	
NO HEDDLES		X		X		O		O		X

O DARK   X LIGHT

A dotted or tear drop effect occurs when the dark color is threaded for two rows, then the light color is threaded for one row. This is repeated across the belt until it's all warped.

The draft shows how the loom is warped.

A chain design on a light background appears when you warp two dark threads and then one light thread where you want the chain to appear.

This variation of the chain design is made by simple planning of where you want your chain effect to fall.

This draft shows how to warp the loom for a chain effect.

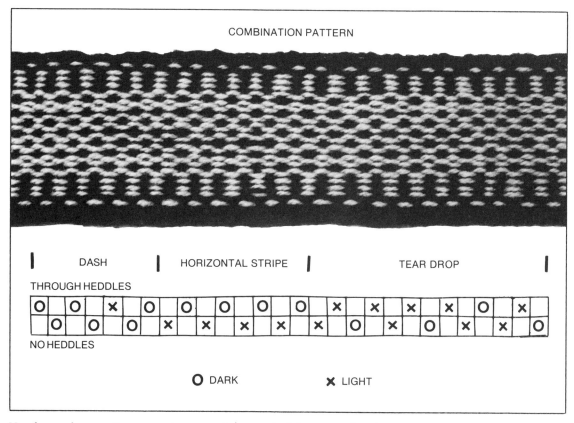

Handsome, busy patterns can incorporate several of these motifs. The draft shows how the belt can incorporate three different patterns.

Weaving the Belt

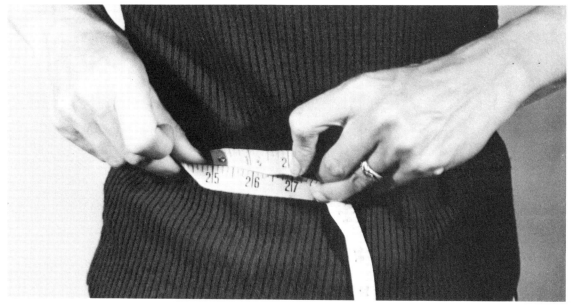

Now plan your own pattern draft. After you have warped your design, start weaving 15″ from the knots at bar 6 to allow enough fringe for the ties. Measure your waist and subtract 2″ to get the number of inches that you'll weave. After weaving, cut the piece off the loom at the knots.

Finishing the Ends

The simplest way to finish the ties is to divide the long fringed ends into four groups and then braid them.

The braids are then tied at the waist for the tight bodice effect.

Another method for finishing the ends of the belt is to fold back the braids to form loops. Cut the braids 2½" long, fold them back, then tuck the ends under a piece of bias tape and sew it down. This gives you four loops on each side of the belt.

Make a long braided tie to lace through the loops.

The finished belt has a casual, peasant look.

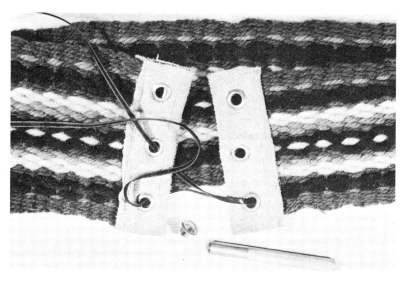

Scraps of suede sewn over the cut ends of the belt is yet another way to make a laced bodice. Grommets were punched through the suede, and leather lacing adds the finishing touch.

8 Color Ideas: Curtain Ties

Designing curtain ties is a good project for color experimentation. Before you begin the project, consider all the color options that are open to you.

Compare a color combination to a musical composition. For a piano piece, a two- or three-note chord can be effective, but for a symphony you need a whole orchestrated score. A beginning student would never write his first composition in full orchestration, but would always be adding to his knowledge so eventually his pieces would become more complex. The same things are true for the weaver—beautiful color can be very simple or quite complicated in concept.

Color

For the weaver, color is one of the most important design factors, and understanding the basics of color can be of invaluable help when you're designing a pattern. There are three basic variables to work with in color.

Value, which describes the amount of white or black which is added to a color. The photo nearby shows a full range of color val-

The *value* of a color indicates its lightness or darkness.

ues, from very light to very dark. *Intensity* describes the brightness or dullness of a color, for example, an apple green as compared to an olive green. *Hue* is the name given to the basic color, such as red or blue.

These variables affect one another just as some notes sound harmonious with one note and discordant with others. If you tried to make a harmonious arrangement out of many opposites—light and dark, bright and dull, or several hues—you would find balancing these elements quite difficult. It's much easier to pick only one aspect of color to work with.

If you wanted a dark and light color combination, a dark, medium, and light blue for example, then your contrast would be in value. If you picked a bright contrasting color combination, such as pink, yellow, and light green, your contrast would be in hue. You wouldn't see a difference in intensity because they're all bright colors.

A *color wheel* is another handy device used in color theory (see diagram below). The primary colors, red, yellow, and blue are equidistant on the wheel. As they mix with their neighbors, intermediate shades are created. Yellow and blue produce green, blue and red produce violet, and red and yellow produce orange. Colors that are directly across the wheel from each other are called complementary colors.

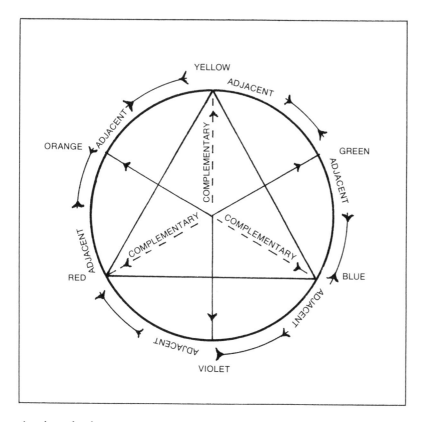

A color wheel.

Bright Color Combinations

Complementary colors of the same intensity make a very vibrant combination. The commercial world often uses this idea to catch our eye. Howard Johnson's blue and orange buildings look clear and sparkly. Texaco's red and green signs copy nature's clue—red holly berries against green leaves.

A color also appears bright when it's surrounded by neutrals or dull colors. In a stained glass window, the black line of the lead accents the brightly colored glass. Try alternating a neutral color with bright colors on a striped belt.

Large areas of color give a brighter effect as well. If the color areas are small, then the dots of color may mix with one another visually. A spot of blue next to spots of yellow give a greenish appearance. The Impressionist painters used this theory to create luminous color effects. When any color is mixed, however, it becomes duller than the original color. A tear drop pattern of red and blue will create a purple-looking area; a wide stripe of red next to blue will retain the original color and brightness.

Softer Color Combinations

Colors that are close to each other or analogous on the color wheel tame each other and often make a pleasing combination. Blues next to greens, or purples next to reds are good examples. Colors close in values, all light or all dark, are also possible combinations. Colors that are of the same hue, or monochromatic, but that have different values are safe choices.

Wrap yarns around an index card to see how colors react to one another.

Experiment With Colors

Often the most handsome combinations are found through experimenting rather than through intellectualizing. Look through your yarns and pick out those you intuitively feel look well together. Wrap these around a folded index card and tape the ends down in back. Now change the proportions of the same colors and see how this changes the effect. This is a good method for picking inkle warp colors.

Look to nature for possible color combinations. The colors on a butterfly, a bird, or leaves against the sky may catch your eye. Analyze what you like about the combination and then try to apply the colors to weaving.

Choose your colors for the use or function of the piece you are weaving. Do you need a color accent or something that blends in with the surroundings? Will dirt and finger marks affect the weaving, or can you choose light colors?

Weaving Curtain Ties

Work out three color combinations which would harmonize with your curtains. Analyze each combination, pick the one you like best, and weave enough of a band to go around both curtains.

After you've woven your band, cut it in half. Put each band through a curtain ring, then sew the cut ends together so that each band forms a circle. The tie will catch up the curtain and can be hung on a hook by the ring.

The finished curtain tie.

9

Dyeing Your Yarn:
A Tie-Dye Belt

Dyeing your own yarn colors can greatly multiply both design and color possibilities. Yarns often come in a small selection of colors and just the right shade is missing, so dyeing your yarn makes any shade available.

Preparing the Dye

Possible dye sources are natural dyes, such as golden rod or onion skins, home dyes found at the five-and-dime store, or commercial dyes such as Ciba and Keystone which are available through the sources listed at the end of this book. These commercial dyes are preferable for their color fastness and brilliance, and to use them you'll need the following materials:

1. Canning kettle
2. Measuring spoons and cup
3. Nonporous rods for stirring (glass or plastic)
4. Rubber gloves
5. White vinegar or 56% acetic acid
6. Non-iodized salt
7. Dish detergent
8. Candy thermometer
9. Cheesecloth
10. Wool

Soak 1 lb. wool for twenty minutes in room temperature water mixed with 1 tbsp. liquid detergent. Then prepare the dye bath. Mix 1 tsp. dye in either 2 tsp. 56% acetic acid or 1 cup vinegar. Lighter shades can be obtained by adding less dye. Add the acid and dye mixture to 1 cup hot water. *Never add water to acid.* Stir well, working out all the lumps of dye. Sift the dye solution through several layers of chessecloth into 4 gallons of water heated to 110°. Add ¼ cup salt, stir well, and add your wool.

Over a half-hour period, bring the wool in the dyebath to just under 210° but don't let the water boil. Then simmer the dye bath for a half-hour. If any color remains in the dyebath, you can add another tsp. acetic acid or ½ cup vinegar to exhaust the dye and then simmer another 15 minutes. Rinse the wool in very hot water, adding cool water a little at a time until finally the rinse water is clear and lukewarm. Let the wool dry, but be sure not to use the clothes dryer or direct sunlight.

Keep some samples of dyed yarn for future reference.

Tie-dyeing

To obtain an interesting, non-geometric pattern in the warp, you can dye a design right into the wool. This is a form of the popular craft of tie-dyeing.

Dyeing the Yarn

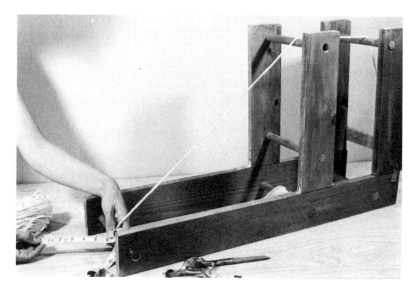

1. Measure the exact length of one warp thread and then add 6″ to the length for knots and shrinkage. Cut 30 pieces of white 6-ply rug wool this length.

2. Bundle the pieces and tie the group of yarns at both ends.

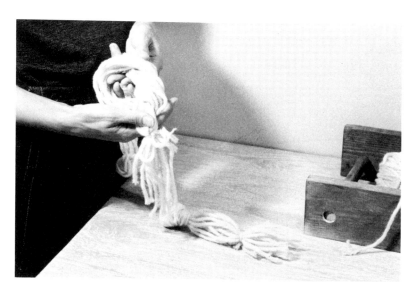

3. Treating the bundle as if it were one thread, tie several overhand knots in it.

4. Then take extra pieces of wool and wrap them around other areas tightly.

5. First soak the wool in water for 10 minutes, then dye the yarn a solid color according to the package directions. Let the wool dry with the ties and wrappings still in place.

6. Take out half of the knots and wraps when the bundle is dry, and then tie and wrap the bundle in a few new places. Re-dye the bundle in a darker dye of a color that harmonizes with your first choice. After you've dried out the bundle a second time, remove all the knots and ties. You'll see you have white, the original dye color, the second dye color, and a color mix of the two dyes.

Weaving the Belt

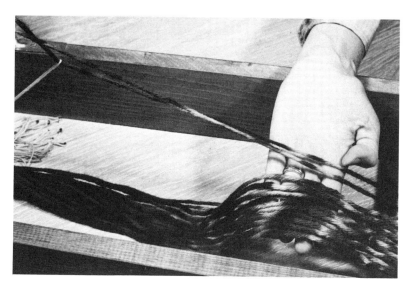

1. (Left) Now warp your loom, but tie on each warp strand one at a time at both the beginning and end of each strand. Take care to line up the color pattern as carefully as possible. Then weave your belt.

2. (Below) These first experiments were achieved through trial and error. With the understanding of the process, however, you can achieve handsome controlled designs in several colors.

10 The Rya Technique: Decorative Bell Hangings

A decorative bell hanging can serve as a bright spot in any home. The metal texture of bells makes a nice contrast with the texture of yarns and this contrast can be accentuated by the rya technique, a method of knotting often used in rug making. The first hanging uses a heavy yarn and a cowbell for decoration. The second incorporates several camel bells, and the third variation uses Christmas bells. They all make great gift ideas.

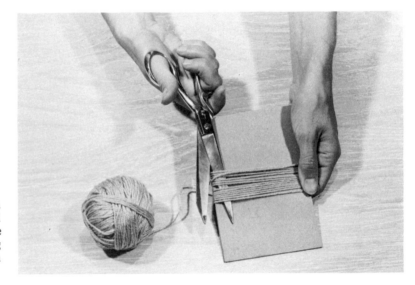

1. First wrap a bit of the yarn around a piece of cardboard 2½" wide. Cut the yarn at one edge of the cardboard giving you several 5" pieces of yarn to work with.

2. Warp your loom with a solid contrasting color about 1½" wide and weave 6" with the same color. Then take two of the short pieces of yarn and place them on top of the two warp strings furthest to your left.

3. Now slip the ends of the pieces up through the center of the two warp strings.

4. Bring the ends all the way through towards you.

5. Pull gently on the ends to bring the knot down close to the weaving and to secure it. Skip the next two warp strings and make another knot.

6. Make knots all across the row, skipping two warp strings between each knot. When you've finished, trim the ends of the shag.

7. Weave three new rows of weft.

8. Make a new row of rya knots, but this time skip the two warp threads at the left, making your knot around the second pair of warp threads. Continue across the row as you did before. Make five more rows of knots in the same manner. You might mix colors and textures of yarns in your knots. When you've finished the knotted section, weave a 7″ section of plain weave. Then make another knotted section of about three rows. Do another 4″ of plain weave and cut the weaving from the loom.

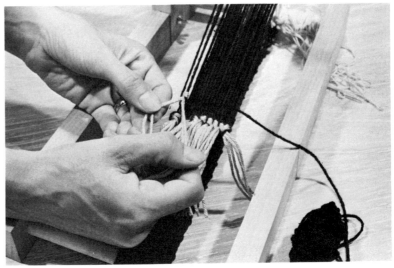

9. Machine stitch the ends of your weaving above the fringe.

10. Sew the top of your weaving around a ring and attach a cow bell to the bottom.

Camel Bell Hanging

1. If you prefer to use several smaller bells instead of just one you can incorporate camel bells into a hanging. In this design you'll need to weave three narrow inkles at the same time. Each narrow inkle band can be a different pattern and color.

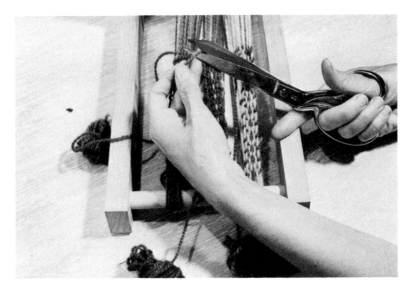

2. After 5″ has been woven, cut the weft yarn of the center inkle close to the edge.

3. Use the weft yarn from the inkle on the far left as the weft yarn for both the middle and the left-hand bands. The far right band keeps its own weft for another 4″.

4. Cut off the far right weft thread and continue weaving the three bands with the one weft thread for as many inches as you'd like. Add some rya knots to the weaving if you like. The finished hanging shows the narrow bands cut off to three different lengths and sewn around the handles of the bells.

Christmas Bell Hanging

Sew Christmas bells on a woven band to add holiday sparkle to a room.
The top fringe becomes the bow that holds the greenery in place.

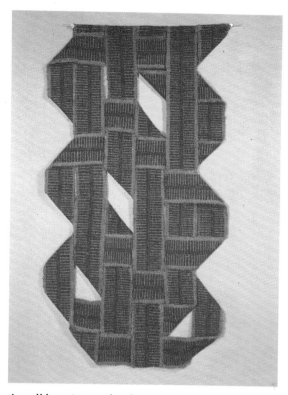

A wall hanging made of interwoven inkle bands as shown in Project 13.

The finished handbag that was made in Project 9.

These belts were designed in adjacent hues, as explained in Chapter 8.

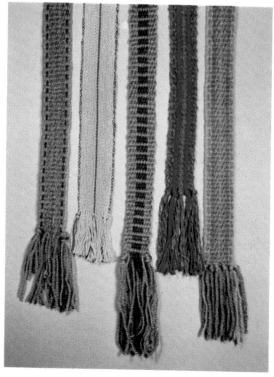

Complementary colors, discussed in Chapter 8, accentuate these belts.

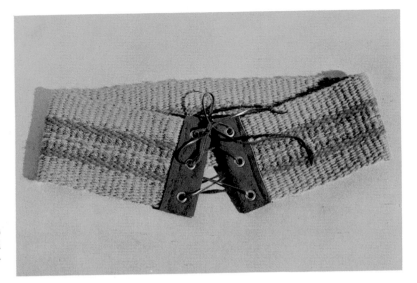

Project 1 shows you how to make this wide belt finished with suede and leather lacing.

The finished, scratch-free eyeglass case that was made in Project 5.

How to make a wider fabric, such as this pillow, is explained in Project 17.

Experiment with color ideas when weaving curtain ties, shown in Chapter 8.

Chapter 9 shows how tie-dyeing can enhance your inkle bands.

Rya knots liven up these bell hangings. The techniques are shown in detail in Chapter 10.

Balsam bags, as shown in Project 10, make great gifts or items to sell.

Liven up a guitar by making an inkle strap for it. Project 2 shows you how.

Project 15 demonstrates how to make a hanging that will move in the breeze.

Inkle border designs are sewn on placemats in Project 11. Pottery by Bill Klock.

Fill in a wooden screen with inkle bands as shown in Project 14.

You can even make a man's tie with an inkle loom. Project 4 shows you how.

Making a poncho is demonstrated in Project 12.

Another variation of the poncho, a "quechque-mitle," is also shown in Project 12.

Project 12 also shows how to make a pullover vest.

A campstool seat made from inkle bands from Project 7.

Project 8 shows how to decorate a director's chair with woven bands.

Christmas tree swags are easily made on the inkle loom. This wrapping technique is demonstrated in Project 16.

PROJECTS

Belts for Different Occasions

1

The use planned for a belt will determine your color choices, the width of the stripes, and the textures you pick. Keep in mind the discussion of yarn textures in Chapter 6 and design belts for various occasions.

Rayon yarn has a lovely sheen so it works very well for a more formal belt. This belt, in three colors, has 22 warp threads. It measures 1½″ in width and was made with rayon rug yarn bought at the five-and-dime store.

The fine, smooth texture of this belt gives it a dressy appearance. It was worked in three colors of pearle cotton #3, has 48 warp ends, and is 1½″ wide.

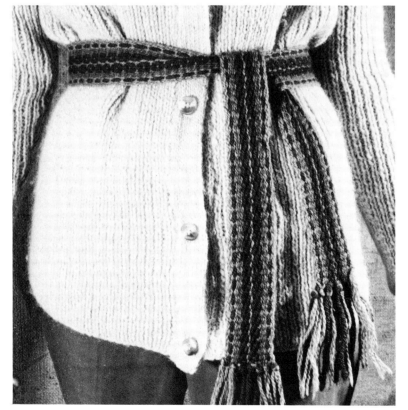

(Above Left) This belt was made with natural jute and green garden twine, both bought at the hardware store. There are 22 yarn ends in the warp, making a belt 1″ wide.

(Above Right) Seine twine and cotton macramé cord in white and navy create a belt with a nautical look.

This belt was made with medium and heavy weight wool bought through yarn companies.

2 Guitar Strap

Perhaps you know a guitarist who would like a guitar strap. Practice making designs with drafts, and choose one that will please the owner of the guitar. Cotton is a good fiber to use because it's strong and smooth.

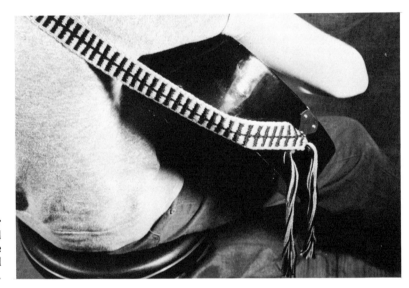

1. Once you decide on color and pattern, weave a band that measures 45″. The fringe at one end is knotted around the bottom peg of the guitar.

2. The fringe at the other end is tied under the strings near the tuning pegs.

3. The finished product is comfortable, attractive, and practical.

3 Headbands

Create headbands in several different styles. The first type of headband is made by weaving a cotton inkle band 2″ wide. The length of the band should be 2″ smaller than the circumference of your head.

Turn under the edges of the band, at the same time encasing a piece of elastic about 3¾″ long and ¼″ wide under the edges. Sew the edges down firmly.

The elastic holds the band firmly in place.

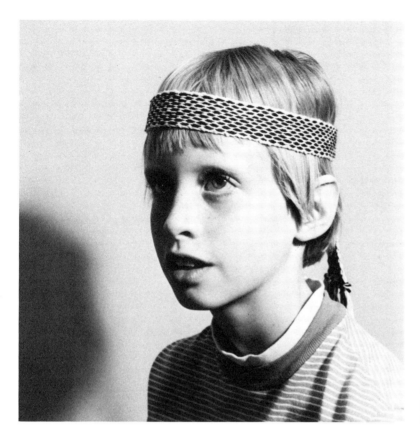

One variation is to use a narrow cotton band, Indian style.

If you have long hair you can combine an inkle headband with your hairdo. Leave long fringes on a 10″ band of weaving and braid the fringes together with your hair.

4 Weaving a Man's Tie

Practice your skill with color and pattern while you weave a man's tie. A 3½" tie made with #3 pearle cotton requires 110 warp ends. Because of the number of warp yarns, the narrow part of your tie, which is knotted, will always be a bit bulky. Ties over 3½" are therefore impossible to weave—more warp threads would make an even bulkier knot.

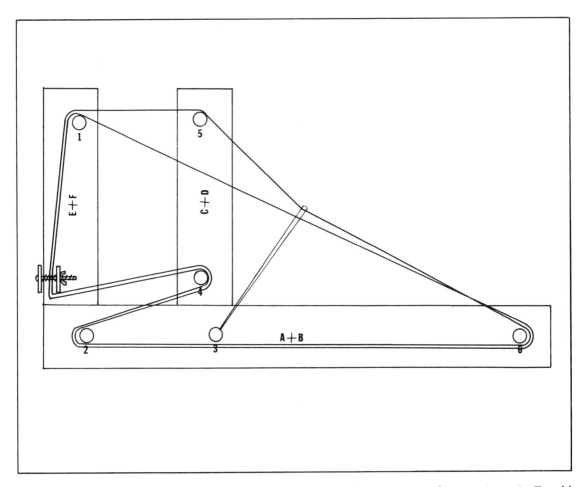

1. You'll need to add extra length to your warp for weaving a tie. To add the extra length, warp your loom as usual, going around bar 1 and then through the tension adjustment. Keep the warp as loose as possible because there will be quite a bit of "take up" in such a long warp. Now pass the warp around bar 4, then back to bar 2 and on to bar 6, as shown in the diagram.

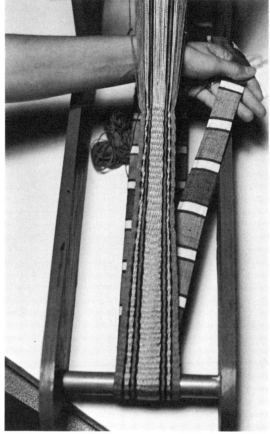

2. (Above Left) Continue warping your loom on this path until you have the required number of warp threads.

3. (Above Right) Use a favorite tie as a pattern for the shape of your woven tie. Place the pattern tie under your weaving and as the tie narrows, pull your weft yarn together so that your edges conform to your pattern.

4. To finish the tie, stay stitch the ends with a sewing machine. Now roll and handstitch the hems at both the narrow and the wide end. Or, if you prefer a pointed end, fold the wide end under to make a point and sew the turned in edges by hand.

5 An Eyeglass Case

Eyeglass cases can make wonderful gifts, are usually highly saleable, and two or three may be woven on one warping. Warp for a piece 2¾″ wide. If you're using 6-ply rug wool, then 36 warp ends are needed.

1. After you've woven the entire length of your warp, cut it into 12″ lengths and machine stitch the cut edges. Roll under the cut edges and hem them by hand.

2. With yarn and a large needle, sew up the sides of the case.

3. Tuck your glasses away in this scratch-free case.

6 A Belt in Leno Lace

The leno weave is both a simple and effective technique for making a lacey belt. For a 1½″ wide belt, warp 18 ends of 2-ply, medium-weight wool in a solid color. Then weave 3″ with the same color. Don't pull the weft yarn tightly as you're weaving, but rather let it show through the warp.

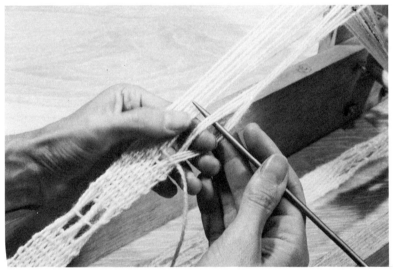

1. Now count six yarns from the right and pull the last three yarns over the first three yarns. Push the group now on your right down with the tip of your finger and pick up the set now on the left with a knitting needle.

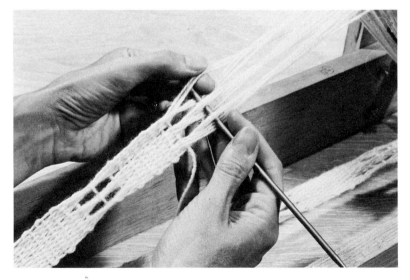

2. Count six more yarns and pick up the three crossed-over yarns with the needle in the same manner as before. Do the same to the last set of yarns.

3. Insert your shuttle in the space held by the knitting needle and pull the shuttle through as you would in weaving.

4. Weave a plain weave above the leno lace area for another 3″.

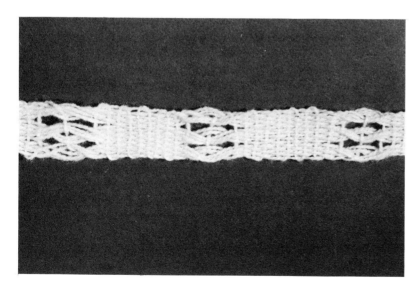

5. Your final result will look like this. It will look a little different on the loom, however, because then it's under tension.

7 A Campstool Seat

A campstool can be an attractive and versatile piece of furniture. Footstool, suitcase rack, and extra seat are all folded into one. Discount and five-and-dime stores usually carry a supply of campstools.

1. The basic campstool.

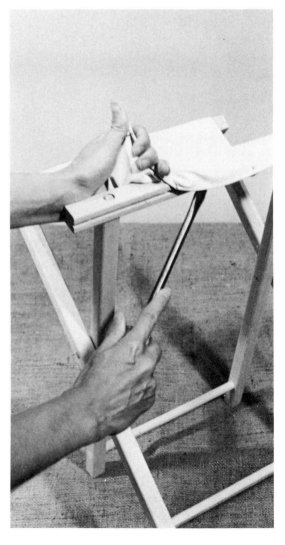

2. Remove the canvas cover from your stool.

3. Stain and varnish the legs to make the wood more compatable with the rest of your furnishings.

4. Weave enough cotton inkle bands of your own design so that you can cut five pieces 21″ long. Then stay stitch the ends of each piece of weaving.

5. Attach the bands to the upper side of your stool with a staple gun or carpet tacks. Wrap the inkles once around the frame and carry it to the other leg. Attach the inkle in the same way to this side.

6. Your new piece of furniture may not be elegant, but chances are you would now accept it in the living room.

7. If not, take it back to the work room and use it for an inkle loom stand. It works beautifully.

Slip Covers for a Director's Chair

8

You can decorate many other furnishings with inkle bands. Make a lampshade, a light cord, a bell pull, or even slip cover a director's chair.

1. Measure the length and width of your director's chair to determine the width and length of the bands you'll need. Add 2″ hem length to each strip for the seat and a 6″ hem allowance for the back pieces.

2. Sew 2″ wide strips together for the back piece. A zigzag machine stitch is ideal.

3. Using your old cover for a pattern, hem the ends of the back piece so it will slip over the back uprights.

4. Slip the new back support in place.

5. Hem all the seat pieces. Leave enough space so that the dowel that holds them in place can slip through. If your new fabric is too bulky, cut some ⅛" welding rod to replace the dowel. This allows more room in the groove for the new material.

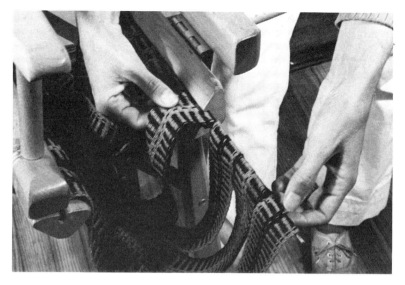

6. Slip the hemmed strips onto the rod.

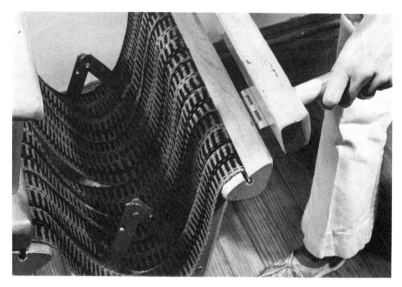

7. Put the seat in place.

8. Weave more inkle bands in and out of the seat and hand sew the ends. This adds reinforcement as well as a bold design.

9. Here is your completed chair.

Handbags

9

Experiment with more inkle designs while you make a handbag. These illustrations show one idea, but interpret the suggestions to fit your own ideas. Inkle bands will adapt to many styles of bag, and design and color are limited only by your imagination.

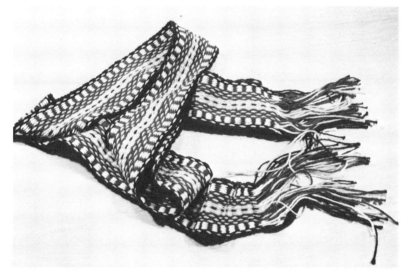

1. Weave a band 2¾″ x 63″ out of 4/4 cotton warp. It will take 58 warp ends. Then make a second band identical to the first.

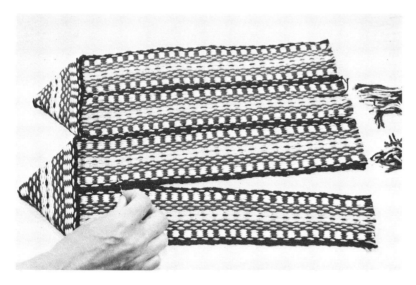

2. Cut each band in half and stay stitch the cut ends. Fold two of the cut pieces as shown in the illustration. Sew the three seams together by hand or with a zigzag machine stitch. This makes one side of your bag.

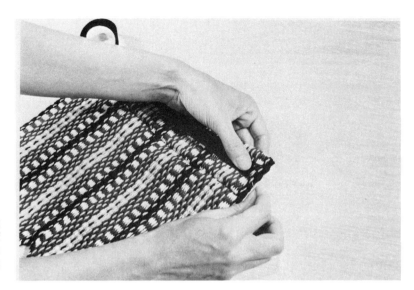

3. Fold over the cut ends and sew a 1½″ hem. Attach 11″ of Velcro tape to your hem edge. Repeat this for the back side of your bag.

4. Weave a third band using the same colors as your first ones, but use a simpler design. Keep the fringed edges as they are. Sew this band to the front of your bag for the handles and sides.

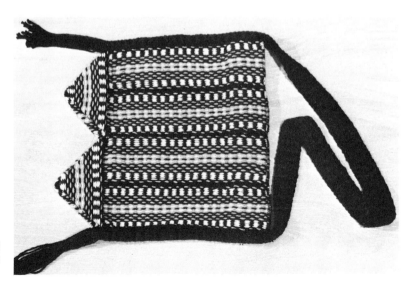

5. Sew the back of your bag to the side band to finish the handbag.

Pin Cushions and Balsam Bags

10

By using cut scraps of wide inkles, you can make pin cushions and balsam bags to give as gifts or even to sell in gift stores that feature small items.

1. Cut your inkle band (about 3½″ wide) into squares. Sew two of these squares together on three sides.

2. Turn the pillow cover inside out and stuff if with wool yarn scraps. Sew up the fourth side by hand.

3. (Right) You now have a saleable product.

(Below) You can make the balsam bag in the same way, but substitute balsam needles for yarn when stuffing. Attach some small pine cones to a corner with a bow of yarn. The bag is shown on a sprig of balsam.

Border Designs

11

Pep up your wardrobe with inkle bands. Blue jean cuffs, shirt pockets, collars, blouse yokes, and coat hems are but a few examples of things that can be enhanced with the addition of inkle borders. Household items, such as placemats or curtains, can also be made more attractive.

Perk up your dinner table by sewing inkle bands onto plain placemats.

Usually you'll want to wash your clothes rather than dry-clean them. Be sure you pre-wash your inkles under the same conditions (hot or cold water) as you do your clothes before you sew the inkle to your material. Then sew on the band either by machine or by hand.

Dress up a skirt and vest with your inkles.

Clothing Designs

12

Styles change from year to year and season to season—suspenders are "in" one year and cuffs another. Keep an eye on what's new in fashion and design something to wear made from inkle bands.

You have made several pieces by combining or sewing together inkle bands. Notice how the pattern you use makes a new kind of pattern as it repeats. In the handbag design, the dark edges became very dominant when sewn together. When you know pieces will be joined, try to visualize how the repeat will develop. Will the width of the stripes become monotonous? Will a big change in value be too distracting?

Here are directions for three types of clothing. See if they inspire you to work out your own patterns. Perhaps you can also design and make a skirt or a vest.

A Poncho

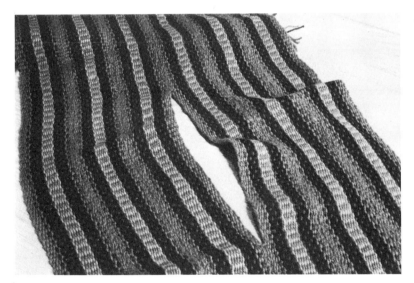

1. To make this poncho, weave six bands, each 3″ x 46″, plus a 6″ fringe at both ends. Sew the bands together, except for 14″ in the middle for the neck hole.

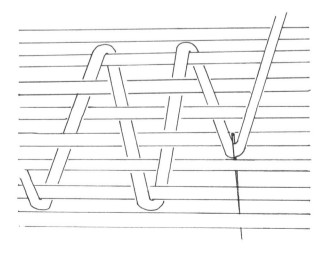

2. Sew the bands together with a machine zigzag stitch, or for a neater appearance, sew by hand to catch the yarns of both bands.

3. Sew small braided ties 8″ from the bottom edge—two on the right side and two on the left side. These will tie the poncho under the arms.

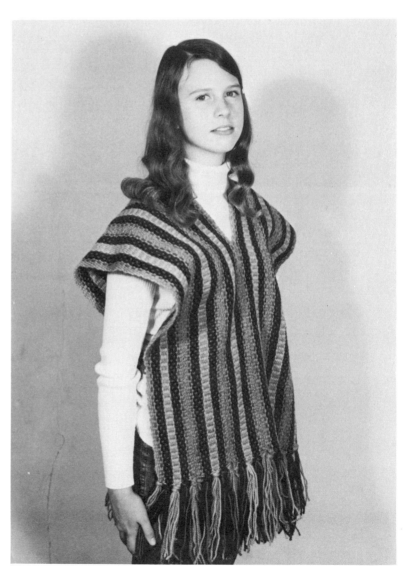

4. Trim the ends of the bands so that they're all even, unraveling some of the ends if necessary. Knot and trim the fringe to finish the poncho.

A Mexican Poncho

1. A quechquemitle is a variation of a poncho design that's popular in Mexico. Sew five bands about 66″ long together in the same manner as for the first poncho. If the bands are unequal in length, cut them the length of the shortest one.

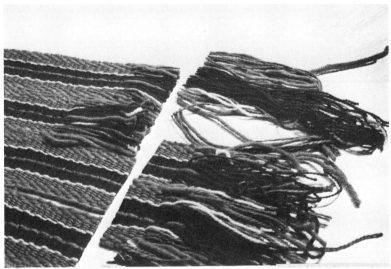

2. Set the cut ends aside for future use.

3. Unravel the woven bands to the length of the shortest one for the fringe.

4. Fold your fabric in half and mark the halfway point with pins.

5. Machine stitch two rows across the fabric, each row ¼″ from either side of the pins. Use large stitches so as not to pucker the fabric.

6. Cut the fabric in half between these two rows of stitching.

7. Place one stitched edge against the selvage edge of the other piece as far down as the fringe.

8. Sew this in place.

9. Fold one of the unsewn edges over as shown in the illustration, making sure the fringes of the folded piece line up with the selvage edge of the other piece.

10. Fold the sewn left edge over to meet the selvage of the top piece and stitch into place.

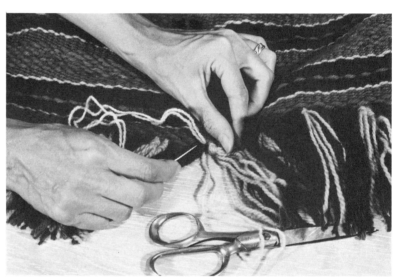

11. Take the cut-off fringes earlier set aside, and sew these around the unfringed edges of your quechquemitle.

12. Enjoy the warmth of your new wrap!

A Pullover

1. For this top you'll need to make one 6″ band 32″ long, one 2″ band 32″ long, and one 2″ band 26″ long, with two pieces of ⅛″ round elastic used as part of your warp.

2. The photo shows the elastic strung on the loom. It's under fairly tight tension to give elasticity to the waist of the top.

3. Cut the fringe off the 2″ x 32″ band and then cut the band in half.

4. Cut the fringe off the 6" x 32" band and then cut the band in quarters.

5. Hem all six cut pieces with bias tape. Your hem length will depend on the measurements of the person you're designing for. It's easiest just to hold the pieces up to the model and pin the proper hem lengths right there.

6. The 6″ pieces will be for the front, back, and underarms of the top; the 2″ pieces form the straps. Measure the waist of your model and sew on the waist band cut to fit these measurements.

Wall Hangings

13

A popular professor of creative thinking started each semester by passing a common brick from one student to the next. He asked each student to name a possible use for the brick. No class failed to find at least twenty uses. The same thing is true of inkle bands, and wall hangings provide a perfect project for experimentation. Inkle bands can be folded, twisted, flat, three-dimensional, fastened, or left free. The long narrow band is really one unit, or module, on which you can build any number of ideas. The following samples show just a few ways to shape your bands. Not all of them were woven on the inkle loom, but all do use the band as a basic unit and should serve as inspirational material.

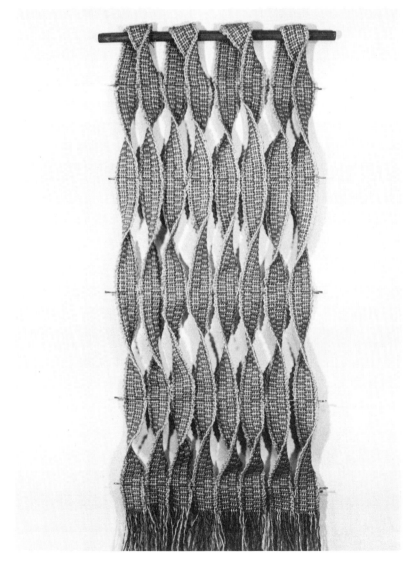

Twisted Hangings

(Above) The detail shows how the brass rod weaves through the jute strips. The hammered flat end prevents it from slipping out.

(Left) Brass welding rods keep the twisted jute bands in place. The perforated face of this piece can produce unusual light patterns if used as a curtain.

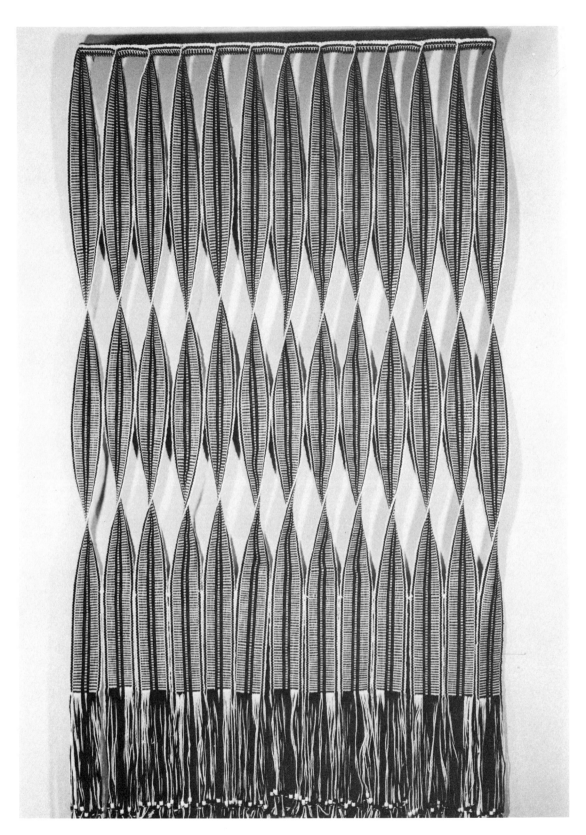

This black and white cotton hanging shows another way to use a twisting theme. Small glass beads weigh down the fringe.

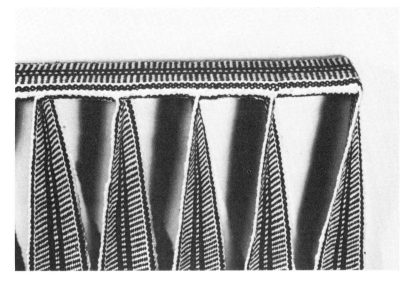

One band covers a lattice molding at the top.

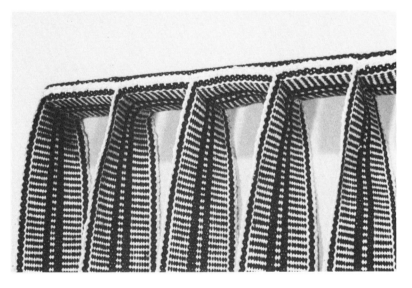

The other bands are sewn to the top band and hang at right angles to it.

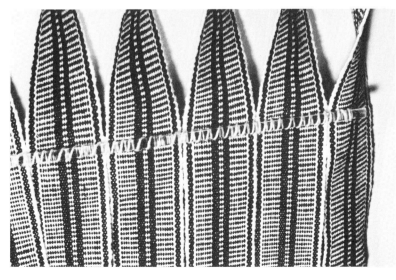

A plastic rod sewn in place on the back side keeps the weaving from curling at the edges.

Intertwined Bands

Three-Dimensional Sculptures

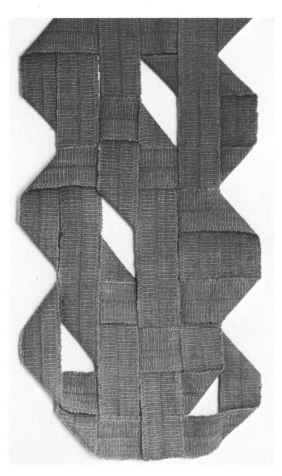

Intertwined woolen bands create this sculpture in low relief.

Mihoko Matsumoto neatly stretches her bands over plastic rods. Note how the bound fringes form the loops.

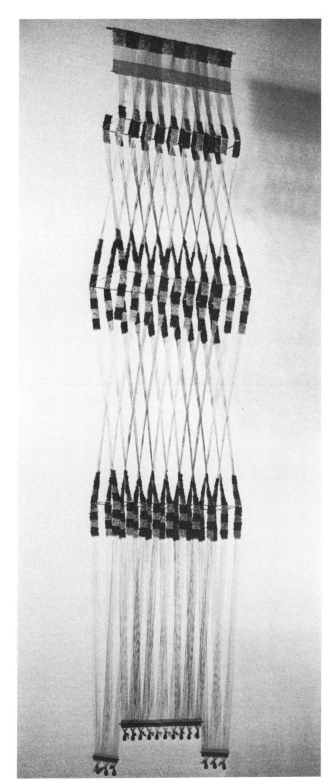
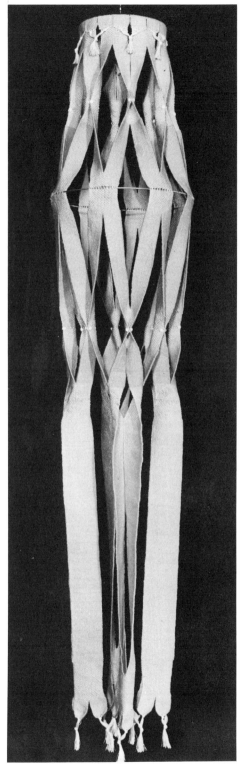

(Left) Terry Illes contrasts woven areas with bare warp threads. She used wool and loop mohair in orange, pumpkin, lime, and peacock for this slit tapestry. (Right) Another piece by Terry Illes shows a sensitivity to structure, form, and detail.

Sculptural Hanging

Marilyn Leon created this free-flowing sculptural hanging with bands woven in paper cord.

The draped bands accent the flexibility of her medium.

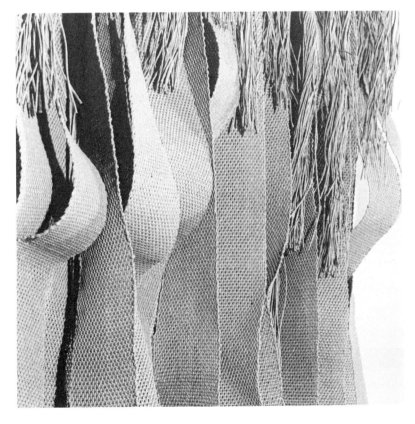

The fringe is an integral part of her design.

123

14 A Room Divider

You've experimented with many design and technique possibilities. Before you start your next project, a room divider, review all the choices you can make as you plan the design.

The structure can be free flowing or architectural, and there are many types of rods, framework, and methods of attachment. Your pattern might be vertical stripes, teardrop, chain, horizontal stripe, or any combination of these patterns. Fibers can include wool, cotton, linen, or paper cord. Color can be of adjacent hues, contrasting hues, value contrast, no value contrast, dull color, bright color, pre-dyed yarn, or tie-dyed yarn. Techniques include warp face, weft face, rya, and lace weave. Texture can be smooth, rough, or mixed.

Now look at the room divider in the first illustration. The uprights on the frame are of 5/4" clear pine, the horizontal bars of ¾" dowels. You need to first plan the correct proportions and the best finish to use. Flat enamel paint was used for this screen.

1. Next you need to decide how you'll design the inkle bands. Will you interweave bands, hang pieces freely, twist bands, or hold them under tension? How will you attach the bands? Do you need to leave hems? Could you leave an inch open in your weaving and weave your dowels into your bands. Should you glue, staple, or sew the bands in place? Should you leave some fringe or not? You can experiment with jute upholstery webbing available at many fabric stores.

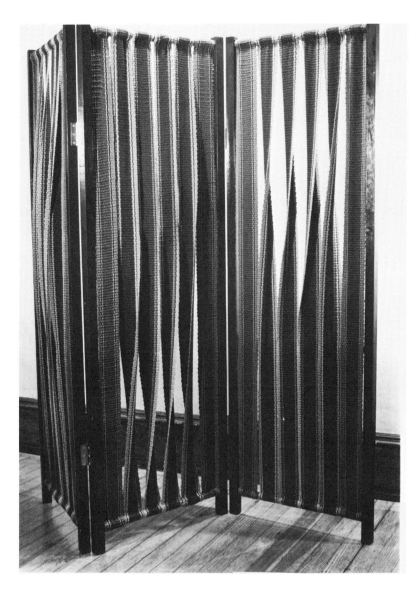

2. You should plan a weaving pattern that will reflect the structure. The contrasting stripes of these bands accent their twist and vertical placement. Pick the correct fiber and texture. Do you wish the yarn to contrast with a sleek wall board? Do you want it to stay as dirt-free as possible? Should it be compatible with other furniture in the room you plan it for? Think about your color choices. Will it be a focal point in your room and demand strong color combinations? Will it be the background for other pieces? How will it look with the rest of the colors around it?

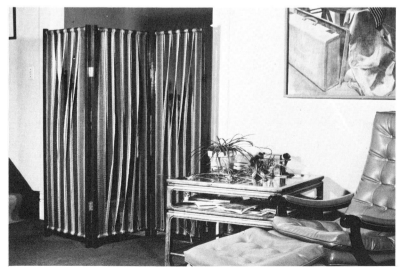

3. Now you can enjoy your divider in its setting.

15 A Hanging That Moves

In contrast to the stable room divider, try using movement as an element in your design. You can see in nature how the movement of leaves, waves, and fire can both excite and hypnotize. Man has played with this idea in fountains and mobiles. You can create a hanging which, like chimes, catches your attention from the movement of the wind.

1. This hanging uses a weft-face technique. Instead of the warp threads creating the pattern, the weft threads are the ones which show.

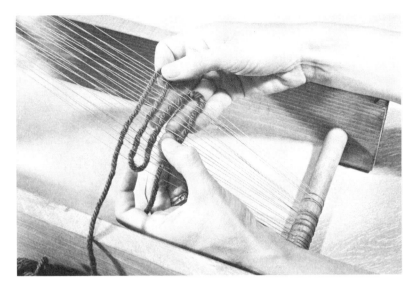

2. Use a fine warp thread or even heavy sewing thread. Weave about four rows with your weft yarn and then stop. Spread your warp threads as evenly as possible across the warp, adjusting it until there are six ends to the inch.

3. Continue weaving, checking often to make sure the position of your warp threads stays as even as possible.

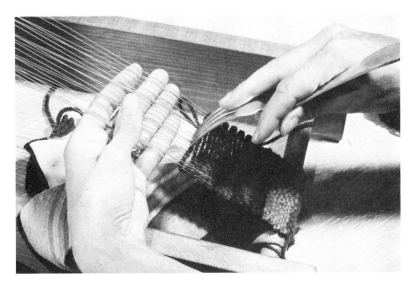

4. Beat the weft yarns down with a fork so they cover the warp. This experimental piece shows different textures of yarn. A rayon yarn from Craft Yarns of Rhode Island (see Suppliers List) was used for the finished hanging.

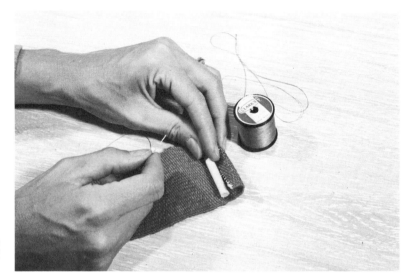

5. Hem one end of each strip around a short piece of wooden dowling.

6. Sew a swivel hook used by fishermen to each hemmed end. This allows your bands to swing freely. Attach the other end of the hook to the edge of a sleeve made from a scrap of weaving. The sleeve should fit over the rod you've chosen.

7. Hem the bottom edges of your bands. To weight the bands, cut and bend some copper foil which will fit over the hemmed edge. Hang your piece in a place where the air circulates freely around it and causes it to move.

Christmas Tree Swags

16

The texture of yarn gives a homespun, good-old-days tone to your Christmas tree and yarn swags are easy to make on an inkle loom. These directions call for 3-ply wool rug yarn, but linen, metallic thread, or jute will give different effects. This isn't really weaving, but a wrapping technique which has many other uses. One weaver threaded many swags on a rod and hung them from her door jamb for a beaded curtain look. Other weavers have wrapped their belt fringes.

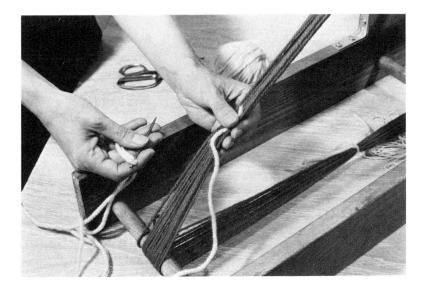

1. Wrap your loom 16 times with 3-ply rug wool but don't bother going through the heddles or tension adjustment. Thread a contrasting color on a large eyed needle. Hold one end of the contrasting yarn firmly against the 16 strands.

2. Wrap the yarn around this end and the 16 strands 14 times.

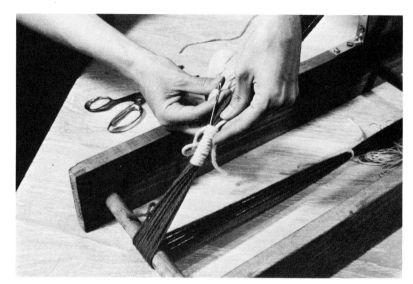

3. Put the needle down into the wrapped area and out the bottom of it.

4. Pull the yarn end firmly.

5. Cut the yarn ends so they don't show.

6. (Left) The finished wrapped area looks like this. Wrap other contrasting colors about every 8″ all along the threads on the loom.

7. (Below) Cut the swag from your loom.

131

8. Drape your swags for a colorful tree.

Weaving a Wider Fabric

17

As discussed in Chapter 2, you can easily increase the width of your loom by replacing your 9″ set of dowels and the tension adjustment with longer pieces. This provides the width necessary to make placemats, scarves, pillow covers, and an endless list of other projects. The loom for the following projects was extended with 12″ dowels.

A Scarf

1. To weave a scarf use a 3-ply wool for the warp. Space the warp about eight yarns to the inch (see Project 15). A mohair weft produces a soft fabric that will feel comfortable next to the skin. As you weave, create the sheds with a stick instead of your hand. When you press up and down on the warp under bar 5, the stick will press the warp more evenly than your hand will on such a wide warp.

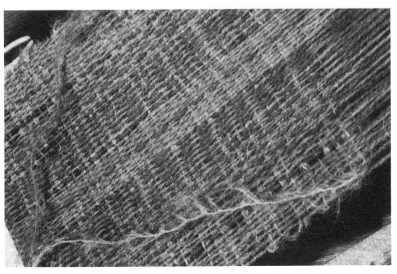

2. You can see that the warp and weft threads both show about the same amount. This is called a 50-50 weave. That is, 50% of the weft shows and 50% of the warp shows.

3. To bring out the softness of your scarf, wash it in lukewarm water. Let it dry on a towel as you would a sweater.

A Pillow Cover

1. A pillow cover is also fun to make with a wider loom. Two covers were cut from one length of weaving.

2. After you sew and stuff the pillow, add tassels made from a few pieces of the cut off fringe.

3. Then tie another fringe yarn around the tassel and clip the ends to the correct length.

Selling Your Weaving

If you are interested in selling your products, there are several things you'll need to know: the laws that affect you as a salesman and a weaver; to whom you should sell your weaving (a store, a fair, the consumer); and how to determine prices. To sell your weaving you should assume the attitude of a professional craftsman and a professional salesman.

Let the much talked about shortcomings of the machine age be your clue to your best assets. How many times recently have you bought a garment that pulled out at a seam, wasn't neatly put together, or appeared in an identical copy the very next day on your neighbor's back? You can make something that's well constructed, won't break or fall apart, and—most important—is one of a kind. Set your own standard for originality, neatness, and craftsmanship. You'll have little competition because quality is a rare commodity.

Fill your orders on time and set consistent prices. Underline your professional image with your own labels, bags, and stationery, but remember these cannot cover up for poor workmanship.

To be a professional businessman you must first learn what legislation applies to you. You're familiar with income tax forms. Conduct yourself as a small business. Keep accurate and full records of your expenses as well as earnings and file both state and federal returns accordingly. You may end up with a profit of only 50¢ when all is tallied, but the bookwork is necessary and not so difficult if you start small.

The U.S. government has definite regulations about labeling. Write the United States Federal Trade Commission, Washington D.C. for copies of: The Wool Products Labeling Act of 1939; The Textile Fiber Products Identification Act of 1960; and The Flammable Fabrics Act of 1954. For a copy of the 1972 Fiber Care Labeling Law write: Care Labeling Rules and Guides, Washington D.C.

All of these laws affect you. If you can't understand the laws after you've read them, write to the U.S. Federal Trade Commission. Chances are they'll answer you by phone.

Become familiar with your state's laws. If you plan to sell directly to the consumer, your department of taxation will license you to collect sales tax.

Many states have some form of upholstery and bedding regulations. Don't sell stuffed pillows without taking special note of this one, because the penalties can be stiff. It's often safest to simply sell the pillow covers without stuffing.

If you plan to sell the products yourself you should ask yourself these questions:

1. Is the community you live in large enough or does it have enough tourist trade for you to sell as much as you wish to? In a city or tourist town perhaps all you need to do is put out a sign.

2. Are you a good salesman? Remember the Rambler ad in which the little man knocks at the door while mumbling "Nobody's

home. I hope. I hope. I hope." If you're embarrassed to be selling something, find someone else to do the job.

3. Do you have a profit too small to share with a middle man?

4. Can you do a good job of advertising your products? Do you have good contacts for commissions?

If the answers to the above questions are yes, you may find a good little business in your own front parlor. For many craftsmen the answers are no. Few like to feel they're trying to push a product on a friend. If your community is small you'll be happiest letting stores beyond your borders handle your products.

There are two different arrangements you can establish with stores. One is that they'll buy "outright." When you give them merchandise, they pay for it immediately. Usually they then mark up the price 100% for their customers. If you sell a belt to them for $4.00, they'll charge $8.00. Craftsmen on the East Coast have an easier time making this arrangement than those living in other locations because stores will often buy in wholesale lots of six or a dozen.

Many stores prefer the second arrangement, to sell your work on commission. They will show your weaving in their store and when your weaving is sold, you get a 20% to 40% commission. This has some advantages, because you can often display a more experimental piece and not have to produce six to twelve similar items for a wholesale price.

How do you approach these stores with your weaving? Make appointments by phone or letter with the "buyer." At your appointment present your work neatly and have definite prices for retail and wholesale arrangements. Mention other sales you've made, as well as satisfied customers you've worked with. The American Crafts Council sells a booklet with names of stores to try.

Another way to contact stores is through craft fairs. These are often profitable for retail customers as well as wholesale. Here the buyer comes to you as you display your wares along side other artists and craftsmen. The craft fair organizers advertise the fair.

Co-ops are another possible outlet for your weaving. Several craftsmen get together, rent a store, and take turns keeping shop and share profits. Just make sure the craftsmen do professional work. It's easy to acquire the image of the little old lady doily-maker.

How to price your weaving is a complicated question. First you need a clear picture of how much you've paid for yarns. Determine how much of a markup will be made, and keep track of how long it takes to make each item. Next take a look at the potential market. Understanding the law of supply and demand is the backbone of good business. You're at an advantage because inkle work often comes in the under $10.00 category and stores prefer this price area for their purchasing. Last of all, or maybe first of all, be fair to yourself; don't undersell yourself or your time. You should make a decent hourly wage. Just because you enjoy your work doesn't make it less valuable to the consumer. Now go out and buy more yarns with all those profits. You've just begun!

Glossary

Beat. to push down against the woven area with hand or shuttle.

Complementary colors. Colors that are opposed to each other on the color wheel.

Draft. A scheme for a woven design, often drawn on graph (squared) paper.

End. An individual warp thread.

Fibers. The hairs or filaments of which yarns are spun.

Harness. An arrangement to hold the heddles, which in turn forms the shed and determines the pattern of the weaving.

Heddle. Loops through which warp ends are threaded.

Hue. The color classification in the spectrum such as red, blue, or orange.

Inkle. A tape, band, or belt.

Intensity. The measure of brightness to dullness in a color.

Leno. Half-twists of warp threads held in place by a weft thread. The result is a mesh or lacy effect.

Ply. The number of threads twisted to form one thread.

Rya. A knotted technique that creates a shag effect.

Selvage. The edge of the fabric bound by the weft.

Shed. A space formed in the warp by the raising or lowering of the heddles through which the weft is passed.

Shuttle. An instrument for holding the weft thread so it can be passed easily through the shed.

Take up. The portion of the warp threads contracted by the weaving. The take-up makes the woven area shorter than the original measurement of the warp threads.

Tension. Stress put on the warp by stretching it tight.

Value. The amount of light or dark in a color.

Warp. The lengthwise threads in the loom into which the crosswise weft yarns are woven.

Web. The part of the weaving that has become fabric.

Weft. Threads woven crosswise into the warp to form the fabric. This is also known as the filler.

Yarn. Fibers twisted into a long continuous strand.

Selected Bibliography

Books

Albers, Anni, *On Weaving*. Middletown Connecticut: Wesleyan University Press, 1965.

Alexander, Marthann, *Weaving—Handcraft: 15 Simple Ways to Weave*. Bloomington, Illinois: McKnight, 1954.

Atwater, Mary Meigs, *Byways in Handweaving*. New York: the MacMillan Co., 1954.

Birrell, Verla, *Textile Arts*. New York: Harper Row, 1959.

LaBarge, Lura, *Do Your Own Thing With Macramé*. New York: Watson-Guptill Publications, 1973.

Articles and Pamphlets

Cendrel No. 330—Metier, Inkle Loom. Quebec, Canada: Nilus Leclerc Inc., L'Isletuille, 1971.

Chapman, Ann, *Weaving with a Loom*. Shelby, North Carolina: *Creative Crafts Magazine*, Lily Mills Co.

The Inkle Loom and How to Use It. Shelby, North Carolina: Lily Mills Co.

Tidball, Harriet, *Weaving Inkle Bands, Monograph 37*. Lansing, Michigan: Shuttle Craft Guild, 1969.

Magazines

Handweaver and Craftsmen, 220 Fifth Avenue, New York, New York 10001

Shuttle, Spindle and Dyepot, 339 North Steele Road, West Hartford, Connecticut 06117

Suppliers List

Dyes

Handcraft House
110 W. Esplande
North Vancouver
British Columbia, Canada

Keystone Aniline and Chemical Company
321 N. Loomis St.
Chicago, Illinois 60607

Straw Into Gold
5550 S. College Avenue
Oakland, California 94618

Labels

Charm Woven Labels
Box 14664 Dept. H.W.
Portland, Oregon 97214

Holiday Gifts
7047 Pecos Street
Denver, Colorado 80221

Yarns

Bartlett Yarn, Inc.
Harmony, Maine 04942

Black Sheep Farm
318 SW 2nd.
Corvallis, Oregon 97330

Butterworth, Charles Y.
Box 3603
Philadelphia, Pennsylvania 19125

Casa de las Tejedoras
1618 E. Edinger
Santa Ana, California 92705

Clasgens Co., J.&H.
Plant #1
New Richmond, Ohio 45157

Condon & Son Ltd., William
65 Queen Street
Charlottetown
Prince Edward Island, Canada

Cottage Crafts
R.F.D. #1
Pomfret Center, Connecticut 06259

Coulter Studios Inc.
138 East 60 Street
New York, New York 10022

Craft Yarns of Rhode Island Inc.
603 Mineral Spring Avenue
Pawtucket, Rhode Island 02862

Filature Lemiex Inc.
St. Ephrem
Beauce
Quebec, Canada

Folklorico Yarn Co.
522 Ramona St.
Palo Alto, California 94301

Fort Crailo Yarns Company
2 Green St.
Rensselaer, New York 12144

Greentree Ranch Wools
Rt. 3 Box 461
Loveland, Colorado 80537

Handweaver
111 E. Napa Street
Sonoma, California 95476

Harrisville Designs
Harrisville, New Hampshire 03450

KM Yarn Co.
18695 Wyoming
Detroit, Michigan 48211

Lily Mills Co.
Box 88
Shelby, North Carolina 28150

Loomery Inc.
210 1st Street
Seattle, Washington 98104

Malsada, Inc., Jeane
Box 28182
Atlanta, Georgia 30328

The Mannings
RD #2
East Berlin, Pennsylvania 17316

Old Mill Yarn
109 Elizabeth
Eaton Rapids, Michigan 48827

Oriental Rug Co.
214 S. Central Avenue
Lima, Ohio

Sandia Studio
620 Sierra Dr. S.E.
Albuquerque, New Mexico 87108

Some Place
2990 Adeline
Berkeley, California 94703

Spider Web
175 N. Main Street
West Hartford, Connecticut 06107

Sutton Yarns
2654 Yonge St.
Toronto 315
Ontario, Canada

Textile Crafts
Box 3216
Los Angeles, California 90028

The Unique
21½ East Bijou
Colorado Springs, Colorado 80902

Yarn Depot
545 Sutter Street
San Francisco, California 94118

Inkle Looms

Cottage Crafts
R.F.D. #1
Promfet Center, Connecticut 06259

Bernard Gordon
M.D., S.C.
2608 W. Farwell Avenue
Chicago, Illinois 60645

Gilmore Looms
1032 North Broadway Avenue
Stockton, California 95205

Leclerc Loom Corp.
Dept. N.H.
Box 491
Plattsburgh, New York 12901

Lily Mills Co.
Shelby, North Carolina 28150

Lieba Inc.
405 W. Franklin Street
Baltimore, Maryland 21201

The Loom Factory
Box 78-H Star Route
Marcola, Oregon 97454

Morgan Inkle Loom Factory
Railroad Engine House
Guilford, Connecticut 06437

School Products Inc.
312 East 23rd Street
New York City, N.Y. 10010

John Seidel
21 Maennecher Avenue
Taftville, Connecticut 06380

Tahki Imports
336 West End Avenue
New York, New York 10023

Willow Cove Crafts
Big Sandy Mush
Leichester, North Carolina 28748

Index

Edited by Jennifer Place
Designed by James Craig and Robert Fillie
Set in 10 point Medallion by Publishers Graphics, Inc.
Printed and bound by Halliday Lithograph Corp.
Color printed by Algen Press Corp.